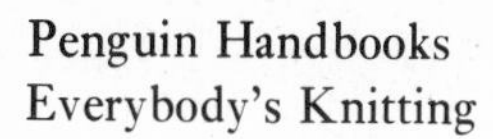
Penguin Handbooks
Everybody's Knitting

Kirsten Hofstätter was born in Copenhagen in 1941. She qualified as a medical secretary and then read psychology and philosophy at the universities of Copenhagen and Montpellier, France. From 1966 to 1969 she worked as an information officer, dealing with aid problems of the Third World, for an international organization and for the Danish ministry of foreign affairs. She then studied to become a social worker in Copenhagen (1972–5) and in 1973 she founded the first women's publishing house in Scandinavia, Honsetryk, which has now published sixteen books, all written by women. She is also working on a forthcoming women's scientific magazine, *Hypatia*, for a Scandinavian forum. She has two children.

KIRSTEN HOFSTÄTTER

EVERYBODY'S KNITTING

Translated from the Danish by Amy Faircloth
Adapted for the English market by Sue Lyons

Illustrations by Grete Rung
Photographs by Martin Rung

PENGUIN BOOKS

Penguin Books Ltd, Harmondsworth,
Middlesex, England
Penguin Books, 625 Madison Avenue,
New York, New York 10022, U.S.A.
Penguin Books Australia Ltd, Ringwood,
Victoria, Australia
Penguin Books Canada Ltd, 2801 John Street,
Markham, Ontario, Canada L3R 1B4
Penguin Books (N.Z.) Ltd, 182–190 Wairau Road,
Auckland 10, New Zealand

First published 1977

Made and printed in Great Britain by
Butler & Tanner Ltd, Frome and London
Set in Monophoto Ehrhardt

Contents

ASE LUND

Introduction

Show me your knitting and I will
tell you what you are like.

Russian proverb

Like all other girls at my school I attended the handicraft class and one of the 'subjects' was knitting. I would have preferred to attend the woodwork course – I enjoyed helping my grandfather with his carpentry – but this was not allowed. The school followed the gospel – still current in some quarters – that boys should be taught carpentry and metalwork and that girls should be taught home economics and handicrafts. Knitting was part of an education to fit girls for their inevitable role as housewives and mothers.

We forget that knitting is an ancient art which in pre-industrial societies was essential to the household's economy; it was not, as it is today, an exclusively feminine hobby to joke about. For example,

both men and women of the mountains of South America knitted caps and ponchoes of brown and white llama wool or brightly coloured sheep's wool with motifs representing characters and incidents from legend. And all round the coast of the British Isles fishermen's families knitted the famous fishermen's sweaters in plain colours, but with intricate cable patterns. Fishnets, diamonds and ribbing – representing a good catch, wealth and happiness – were knitted on the men's sweaters. The women's pattern was the tree of life which promised long life and strong children. Each family had its own particular pattern, which meant that the origin of the wearer was readily identifiable in case of an accident at sea.

These patterns did not come out of a knitting book; they were created by the knitters themselves and handed down through the generations. People enjoyed their knitting, but it was not primarily a hobby. There were no shops selling mass-produced food and clothes; each household had to make its own. Activities like preparing food and making clothes, which are today despised as 'women's work', were essential contributions to the household economy.

The devaluation of these previously essential tasks can be seen in the history of knitting in my native Denmark. Knitting has been known in Denmark since the middle of the sixteenth century, and there are many tales of famous knitters. One such was Ane Bjerg who

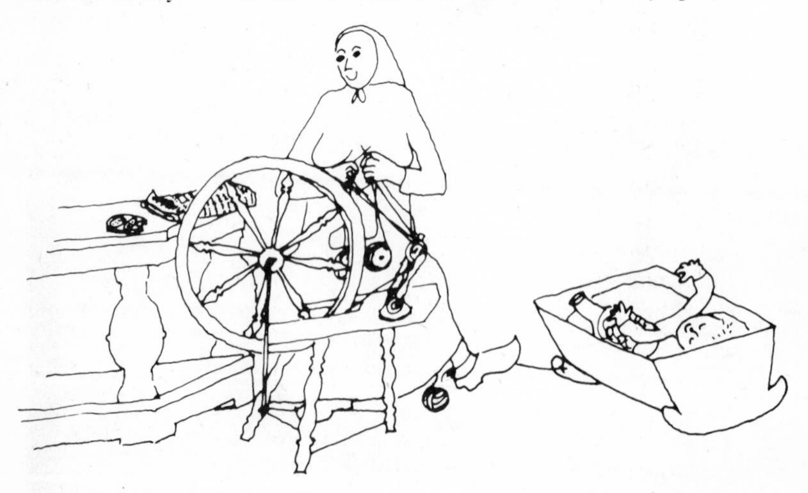

could knit stockings, spin yarn, rock her baby, churn butter, read the newspaper, and eat a sandwich all at once. She could easily guide the yarn with two fingers, leaving eight to knit the socks. She put the cream in the cradle so that she churned the butter and rocked her baby at the same time. As she was so practised at these familiar tasks, she didn't have to watch, but could read the newspaper that lay on the table next to her sandwich. There are stories of male knitters accomplishing similar feats. In the nineteenth century Mikkel Holstener knitted his way to the mill with a sack of flour on his back. There he bought butter and carried it home in his wheelbarrow. To leave his hands free for knitting he tied ropes to his wheelbarrow and dragged it behind him. In Herning about 150 years ago a parish clerk called Pae Sku'el taught three classes in his school room. The children sat at a long table and the clerk's wife sat at the end carding and spinning wool. Pae Sku'el would pace back and forth lecturing and knitting at the same time. Other teachers would knit as they taught, handing the knitting to a member of the class when they wanted to write on the blackboard.

In Jutland there were knitting rooms attended by the whole village, where stories were told and spinning competitions held. Preachers, educated in the cities, fought against the knitting rooms, denouncing them from their pulpits. They alleged that all kinds of immorality took place in the knitting groups and warned that knitting was a female pursuit which softened men so that they could no longer cultivate their fields, but would sit enthralled listening to the old wives' tales told in the knitting rooms. Consciously or unconsciously the preachers saw the knitting groups as rivalling the church as the arbiter of community attitudes. In both church and knitting room men and women met and talked, but the preachers had no control over the latter.

In the middle of the last century when the textile industry developed in Denmark the factories were built where the knitting groups flourished – that is, where the labour force was experienced with textiles. The first knitters to lay down their needles were the stocking knitters from the Herning area who began to use machines. The city remains the centre of the Danish textile industry. Industrialization meant that spinning, weaving and wool dying went to the factories and disappeared from the homes until modern craftsmen and women revived the arts. People still knitted in their homes but it was now 'women's work' to be despised along with cooking and cleaning because it didn't make a profit. And anyway why make your own clothes when you could buy mass-produced garments in the shops? For most people knitting is no longer a creative art because we follow patterns laid down by manufacturers who recommend that we use their particular yarn. We are so unsure of the value of our own work that someone has to tell us what is 'fashionable', how to knit it and what to knit with – and all the time we feel that a machine could probably do it better.

My experience at school in the handicrafts class – where we were expected to knit quickly, neatly and to prescribed patterns – did not encourage my creativity or allow me to enjoy knitting, but when I married and had a baby I wanted to knit clothes. Like all other knitters I used patterns from weekly knitting magazines. I bought ten balls of a specified yarn, since no pattern allowed me to choose what to knit with. As a reward for knitting up fifty balls of yarn I could get the fifty-first free by saving the fifty bands from the balls and sending them to the manufacturers. My getting this free gift meant that I had to plough through patterns like the one for a 'delightful baby suit' with butterfly patterns:

Row: k 2, sl 1 purlwise with yarn at the back, k 1, yon, pass sl st over k 1 and yon (cross st made),* k 6, cross st, repeat from * to the last 2 sts, k 2.

At that time I didn't realize that it was the knitting pattern that was being difficult, not I. So it was many years until I tried to knit again.

By that time I had become involved in the women's movement. I had begun to doubt the authority of those who try to stereotype people into male/female roles without considering people's talents and needs, and I began to doubt the authority of knitting patterns as well. I realized that knitting isn't difficult and that anyone can knit. You don't have to follow a detailed pattern using a particular kind of yarn – it's easy to make up your own patterns.

I put my ideas into a knitting book – *Hønsestrik* (Hen Knit). Following the publication of the first edition in Denmark I received many letters from knitters echoing my own experience. Gudde Fog wrote:

It has always irritated me the way creativity is so limited by the dictates of a knitting pattern. It is also annoying that there are special patterns for certain yarns and much of this wool is more expensive because patterns have been designed for them. Why should I pay extra for a service I will not use?

And a worker at the post office described how the whole office had become involved in her knitting, as must have happened in the knitting rooms of the past:

> Everyone was discussing the motifs I had knitted. There was great disagreement as to whether my hares were really rabbits or whether the rabbit's backside was really a windmill. I was knitting a mystery pullover that would turn out to be the product of suggestions from many different people. It looked very original when finished and we all had a very good time watching it develop.

Two more editions of *Hønsestrik* have appeared in Denmark. They contained patterns knitted by friends and myself plus advice from other knitters.

HOW TO USE THIS BOOK

This English edition – *Everybody's Knitting* – is a combination of the three Danish editions. The book is divided into four parts: first of all a technical section explaining how to knit in rounds, how to make your own designs and how to knit in fairisle. Those experienced in these techniques can skip this section and go straight on to the second part of the book, the patterns themselves. These patterns are not meant to be followed exactly – they are there to inspire you. I have tried to make the instructions as simple as possible, since many people are put off knitting because of the complicated abbreviated instructions in knitting patterns.

The third part of the book gives instructions for those who don't know how to knit at all and would like to learn. This includes instructions for sewing up garments and some simple crochet for edging your knitting.

Lastly, there are names and addresses of suppliers of yarn, and for those who would like to spin as well as knit, a simple method of spinning wool. At the very end there are charts of the motifs illustrated in the photographs for you to copy, and, more important, to inspire you to invent your own.

Finally, my interest in knitting has had some unexpected results. My first book was such a success that I was able to start a publishing house for women. We've published poetry, novels and books on the women's movement. Much more can come of knitting than you might think.

KIRSTEN HOFSTÄTTER
Espergærde, June 1975

A Note on Measurements

With the exception of knitting needles, for which a table is given on page 117, both imperial and metric measurements are given throughout this book. As these measurements are not exactly comparable, use imperial or metric only.

Unless you know what size of knitting you produce with the yarn and needles you are going to use always knit a small sample first to check the number of stitches you need. Otherwise the garment could turn out to be larger or smaller than intended. (See pages 22–3.)

Basic Techniques

The garments in this book were knitted as far as possible in rounds using either a circular needle or a set of four double-pointed needles. My friends and I invented our own designs and knitted them in brilliantly coloured patterns. If you have never knitted in this way you will find the following pages useful; you will discover how to knit on circular and double-pointed needles, how to invent your own designs and how to knit in fairisle.

KNITTING IN ROUNDS

Knitting in rounds or 'circular knitting' produces knitted seamless tubes which can be either sewn or knitted together. The knitting seems to grow more quickly than when you knit each piece separately, and there is very little tedious sewing to do when you've finished. This kind of knitting is done with either a circular needle or a set of four double-pointed needles.

KNITTING ON A CIRCULAR NEEDLE

Circular needles consist of two short needles joined together by a length of flexible plastic wire. They can be bought from chain stores or from specialist wool shops. Circular needles come in the same sizes as regular straight needles – the higher the number on the packet, the thinner the needle. *Be careful when buying circular needles to notice not only the size but also the length.* They range from 16 ins./40·5 cm to 42 ins./107 cm in length. It is important to make sure you buy the correct-length needle because the circumference of the tube you are knitting must be larger than the length of the needle – if it's smaller the knitting will be stretched out of shape. So any knitting you do on a circular needle must be at least 16 ins./40·5 cm in circumference, this being the shortest circular needle available. This means that narrow articles like sleeves, gloves, socks and hats have to be knitted on a set of four double-pointed needles (see page 19). However, you don't need to buy every length of circular needle as the needle will easily accommodate knitting of a circumference three times the needle's length. You therefore only need buy a 16-in./40·5-cm and perhaps a 36-in./91-cm needle. These should hold any tubes you may knit.

Once you have bought your needles you are ready to begin to knit. (For information on yarns see page 109.)

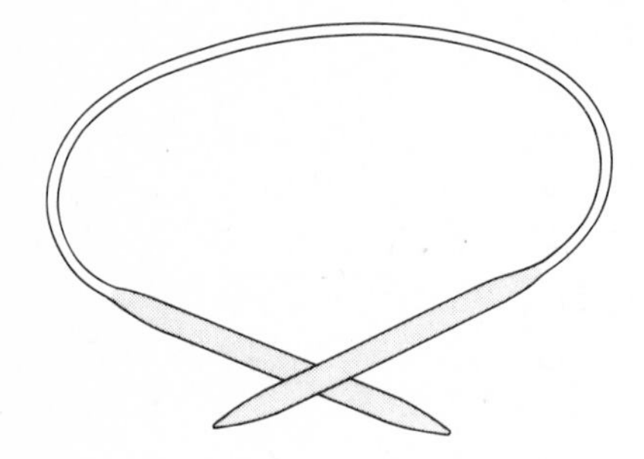

Casting on

Cast on in your usual way; it is easier if you use a pair of regular needles the same size as the circular needle you want to use. When you have cast on the number of stitches required, knit these stitches from the regular needle on to the circular needle. The next steps are to mark the beginning of the round and to join the knitting to make a circle.

Marking the beginning of the round

When you're knitting on regular needles it's obvious where each row begins and ends. However, it's sometimes difficult to see the beginning of a round when you're knitting in tubes. You'll therefore find it help-

ful to have some kind of marker to show where each round begins and ends.

The easiest way to do this is to take a short length (about 2 ins./5 cm) of yarn in a contrasting colour and knot it firmly to make a small loop. Slip this loop on to one end of the circular needle before you join the knitting. Then when you come to this loop on each round of knitting, slip it from one needle to the other. You will thus always be able to see where the round begins.

Joining the knitting

Before you join the knitting make sure that the stitches are not twisted round the needle. Put the needle on to a hard flat surface such as a table and untwist the stitches – it's more difficult to do this if you rest the knitting on your lap. It is very important to remember to do this; if you don't your knitting will be twisted and unwearable, an eternal loop.

When you're certain the stitches are not twisted, bring the points of the needles together. (Make sure the marker is still on one of the needles.) Put the right-hand needle through the first stitch on the left-hand needle and knit it as tightly as you can. Knit the next few stitches tightly too and then knit to the end of the round. You can now begin to knit from the hem of the garment.

Don't worry if you have a few loose stitches where you joined the round. These stitches can be pulled through to the wrong side when you've finished knitting, or you can turn under the first few rows. Besides, as you become more expert in circular knitting you'll become more expert at joining the cast-on stitches.

Working basic stitches

As you knit with a circular needle you will see that the right side is always facing you. Because of this you will use different methods to work basic stitches from those you use when knitting on regular needles.

Stocking stitch. On regular needles stocking stitch is produced by alternately knitting and purling the rows. On a circular needle simply knit every round to produce stocking stitch. If you've never knitted in rounds this is difficult to believe – but try it and you'll be convinced.

Reversed stocking stitch. If you want a reversed stocking stitch effect when knitting on a circular needle, simply purl on every round.

Garter stitch. When working garter stitch on regular needles you knit every row. On a circular needle this would produce stocking stitch.

To produce garter stitch on a circular needle knit one row and purl the next. The purl rounds form the ridges characteristic of garter stitch.

Ribbing. On each round knit the knit stitches and purl the purl stitches to produce a ribbed effect.

Decreasing, increasing, picking up stitches

Use the same methods as you would when knitting on regular needles.

Casting off

Cast off with a circular needle in the same way as with ordinary needles.

Knitting back and forth on circular needles

You'll find that some of the sections of the garments are knitted back and forth on the circular needle. When doing this remember to work the basic stitches as you would when using ordinary needles.

KNITTING ON DOUBLE-POINTED NEEDLES

Double-pointed needles are sold in sets of four. They come in the same sizes as regular needles and look the same except that they are pointed at both ends. They are used for knitting narrow pieces of circular knitting such as gloves, socks, hats and sleeves which wouldn't fit on to a circular needle.

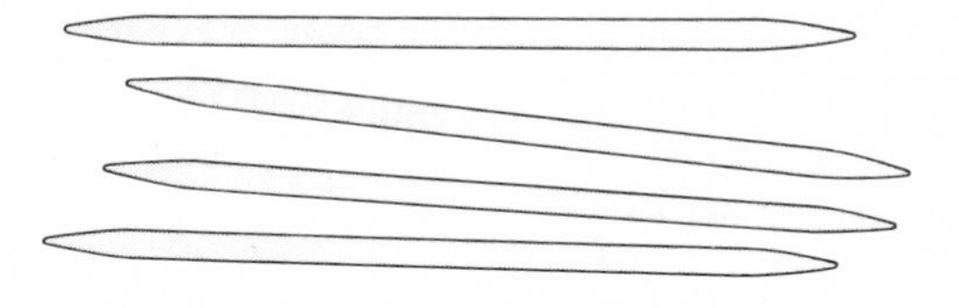

Casting on

Cast on the required number of stitches; you will find it easier if you use regular needles the same size as your double-pointed needles. Knit these stitches on to three of the double-pointed needles, dividing the stitches evenly among the needles.

Joining the knitting

Make a marker to show the beginning of the row and ensure that the stitches are not twisted round the needles, as described for circular needles (see page 18).

To join the knitting bring the points of the first and third needle together so that the beginning and end of the row are together and the needles form a triangle. Using the fourth needle, knit the first stitch on the first needle tightly. Knit the next few stitches tightly and then knit to the end of the round.

Knitting in rounds

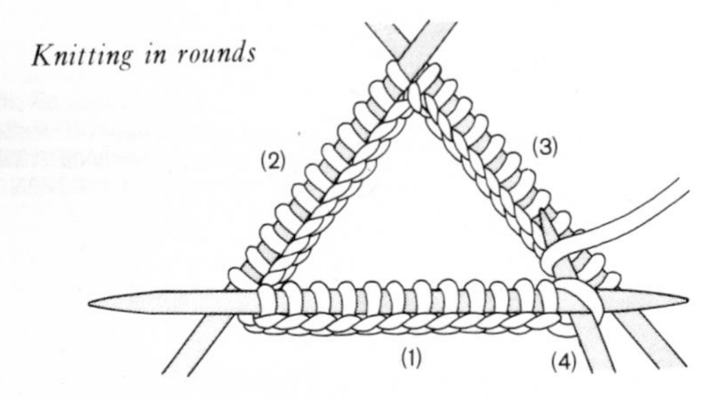

Working basic stitches

When knitting on four needles the basic stitches – garter stitch, stocking stitch, rib – are produced in the same way as on a circular needle, that is, knitting every round produces stocking stitch, knitting and purling on alternate rounds produces garter stitch.

When using four needles the stitches are divided equally between three of the needles and the fourth is used to start the knitting. Starting at the beginning of the round knit the stitches from the first needle on to the fourth needle, which is the free needle. Then knit the stitches from the second needle on to the first needle, which is now free. To complete the round knit the stitches from the third needle on to the second needle, which is the free needle. Continue to work in this way until you have knitted the required length.

Pull the yarn tightly when you finish knitting the stitches on each needle. This will help prevent loose stitches at the join.

Casting off

Use the same method for casting off as you would use when casting off from ordinary needles.

IF YOU ARE A BEGINNER . . .

. . . turn to pages 95–107 where you will find descriptions of basic knitting techniques.

INVENTING YOUR OWN KNITTING PATTERNS

Now that you know how to knit on circular and double-pointed needles, you can learn how to make your own patterns. To do this you must first decide what style of garment you want to make, and then you need to measure the person you are knitting it for.

MEASURING

The measurements you take depend on the garment you want to make – generally speaking you measure the person at the points where the knitting fits the body. For example, for a sleeveless slipover measure the chest; for a sweater measure the arm length, chest, upper arm or elbow and wrist; for trousers, the waist, hips and the widest part of the thigh; for a skirt, the waist and the hips (if it is fitted).

Use a non-stretch fibre-glass tape measure and measure the widest part of the hips, chest, thighs, etc. Make a note of these measurements. If the person you're knitting for isn't there or you want to surprise him/her you can take the necessary measurements from a garment that fits him/her well.

If you invent a pattern you must also decide how long or wide to make the pieces that don't fit the body. For example, how long a pullover or skirt do you want; how wide should you make the body and sleeves if you want a loose sweater; how wide should the fronts be if you want to make a cardigan or coat that crosses to close? Then you must decide on details such as the sort of collar you want, the pockets, sleeve and armhole shaping (ordinary, square, raglan, kimono, etc.); on finishing techniques (knitted-in hems, crocheted edges, for example), and so on.

MAKING A PAPER PATTERN

When you have the measurements you need it's a good idea to make a paper pattern of the garment you intend to knit. Use sheets of brown paper or newspaper. You can then measure the knitting as you go along even if the person you're knitting for isn't around.

WORKING OUT HOW MANY STITCHES TO CAST ON

Once you've taken the necessary measurements and made a paper pattern, you have to work out how many stitches to cast on before you can begin to knit. To do this you must do a piece of sample knitting to gauge your own tension. Some people can't be bothered to knit a sample – they want to get straight on with the garment! I can't stress too much how important a sample is. Unless you know what size of knitting you produce with a certain size of needles and type of yarn, you will have no idea how big your garment will be. Of course if you don't mind a slipover turning into a dress, that's fine. But, things may not always turn out so conveniently: you may find yourself in a garment that swamps or strangles you. And it doesn't take that long to do a swatch.

First of all knit a sample swatch using the yarn and needles you intend to use to make the garment. Cast on about twenty stitches and knit about twenty rows – this makes a fairly large swatch that is easy to measure. When you've knitted about twenty rows, cast off and place the swatch on a flat hard surface like a table and flatten it out. (If you put the swatch on your knees your calculations will not be accurate.) Take a ruler – a clear plastic one is the easiest to use – and measure how many stitches you have knitted to an inch/centimetre. Now multiply that number by the number of inches/centimetres of your measurements. This gives you the number of stitches you should cast on for a skin-tight fit.

However, if you knit in fairisle, with more than one colour, the knitting tends to tighten. So unless you want a really tight fit, you should add enough stitches to give another inch or two, depending on how tight you want the garment to be.

For garments that need more 'ease' because you'll be wearing them over other clothes – such as coats and jackets – you should add enough stitches to make the knitting two to three inches (five to eight centimetres) wider.

You may also need to adjust the number of stitches to make it easier to fit in the motifs when knitting fairisle (see page 26).

Example

To make the above explanation clearer, imagine you want to knit a sleeveless slipover for yourself.

Your chest measurement is 36 ins./91 cm. Having knitted a swatch you find you knit 5 stitches to the inch/2 stitches to the centimetre. Multiply the number of stitches per inch/centimetre by the number of inches/centimetres you measure: for a skin-tight fit you should cast on 180 stitches. However, knitting in fairisle makes the knitting tighter so add another 5 stitches to make the knitting an extra inch/2·5 cm wider. For a perfect fit for knitting in fairisle, cast on 185 stitches.

Finally, don't worry if the knitting still turns out too big or too small. If you discover this when you finish the garment, an original piece of knitting makes a very welcome present; and you can always make the tube into something else if you find out it's the wrong size while you're knitting.

TRAPPE

KNITTING FAIRISLE PATTERNS

INVENTING YOUR OWN FAIRISLE MOTIFS

My friends and I knitted the brilliantly coloured clothes illustrated in this book using patterns invented by ourselves. There are pages of these designs at the back of the book, which we hope will inspire you to invent your own. This is very easy to do.

Decide what motif you would like to knit. Draw the outline on a piece of graph paper and fill in the outline with x's. Each x represents one stitch. It is a good idea to show the different colours you intend to knit on this pattern, preferably by using coloured pencils which will help you to see what your design will come out like. If you have no crayons you can use a combination of x's, o's, v's or A's, B's and C's. You can invent designs from anything – fruit, flowers, animals, letters, etc. You can use some cross-stitch transfer patterns (which are sold very cheaply in needlework shops) as charts to knit from.

When you invent a motif, it's a good idea to try it out first on a sample or swatch. Keep these samples as they make very decorative patchwork when sewn together and provide a permanent record of your invention.

Bear in mind when planning your patterns that it is best to stick to only two different colours in each row or the loops on the back will be very complicated, and tend to make the knitting very thick; that vertical stripes and checks if they are too narrow tend to cause more puckering than other shapes, and that checks and wide stripes need to be woven behind.

Almost anything can be turned into a fairisle pattern. More complicated images work better and are easier to do on a large scale (for example, a face, a house, a landscape, or a word). Small, simple, repeated images are often effective, like, for example, the traditional Norwegian and Fair Isle patterns.

Try using combinations of ordinary stripes and fairisle, or different stitches (for example, garter stitch) and fairisle, or try using fairisle as a border or detail rather than as an overall pattern.

PLACING THE MOTIFS

When knitting a garment in fairisle you can either decide as you go along which motifs you are going to knit or plan the layout for the whole garment in advance – you could knit figures on a theme – rows of fruit or vegetables, for example.

Once you've decided what your first motifs will be, you have to decide how to place them. Whether to space them out along a row or whether to use larger motifs, perhaps just one in the middle of the piece.

If you want to space your motifs regularly you need to count the number of stitches there are in each motif, then decide how many stitches you want to leave between them. Casting on a number of stitches that can be divided by several numbers makes this easier. For example, 180 can be divided by 2, 3, 4, 5, 6, 9, 18 and 20. So if your motif is six stitches wide and you leave three stitches between each motif this gives a total of nine, which will divide evenly into 180. A number like 187 isn't divisible in this way and makes placing the motifs more difficult.

Having decided how many motifs to knit on each row of pattern, mark out two or three of them with x's on graph paper, showing any spaces you have decided to put between the motifs. This will help you to see how to knit the first round of the pattern.

WORKING FROM A CHART

In circular knitting remember that when you are knitting in fairisle from a chart you should knit from right to left of the chart on every round. When you are using regular needles or knitting back and forth

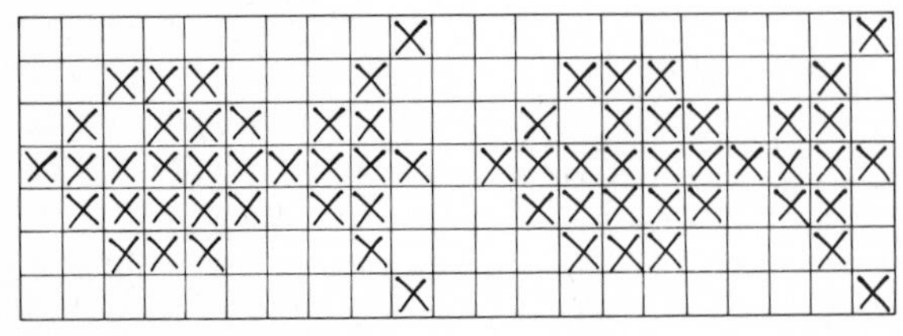

Knitting in rounds

on your circular needle, you should knit from right to left on the right-side rows, and from left to right on the wrong-side rows.

When you are knitting from a chart remember that each x on the graph paper represents one stitch in the knitting, as does one space.

KNITTING SMALL MOTIFS

If the motifs and the spaces between them are less than five or six stitches, the colour you are not using can be stranded loosely at the back of the knitting. But the stranding must be *loose* or the knitting will pucker. Don't forget that the garment will probably be slightly stretched when it is worn. You can 'weave' the different strands of wool together at the back of the work if the strands seem very long. This means crossing the colour you are knitting round the colour being stranded, to catch it in place before it is used again, but avoid doing this if you can as it tends to pucker the knitting, unless you take care to keep the knitting loose. If you're not sure that you're knitting loosely enough try stretching it in your hands. If the figures quickly pull out of shape it is too tight.

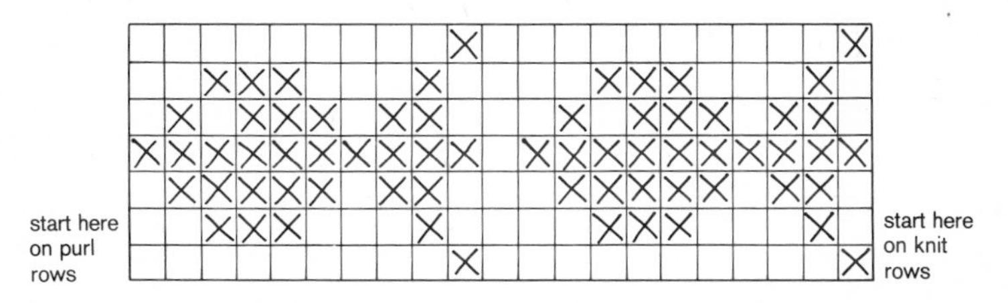

Knitting back and forth

KNITTING LARGE MOTIFS

If the motifs you are knitting are very large, or if you want to put one large motif on, say, the front of a sweater, you can't strand or weave colours as when knitting small motifs. It would waste yarn and give you enormous loops on the inside.

When knitting large motifs you have to knit back and forth on your circular needle to avoid leaving loops, and then sew up the gap caused as for a seam in ordinary knitting. It is best to arrange things so that the seam comes on one side of the body. Remember to read the chart from right to left on the right-side rows and from left to right on the wrong-side rows (see page 27). After you've finished the motif go back to knitting round and round as before.

If you're knitting more than one motif in a row you will have to use separate balls of yarn for each to avoid enormous loops. Keep these balls on the inside of the knitting to stop them tangling with the background colour, which can be kept on the outside.

When you change colours when knitting back and forth in a pattern, put the old colour round the new one before you continue knitting. If you do this the change of colour will not make holes in the knitting.

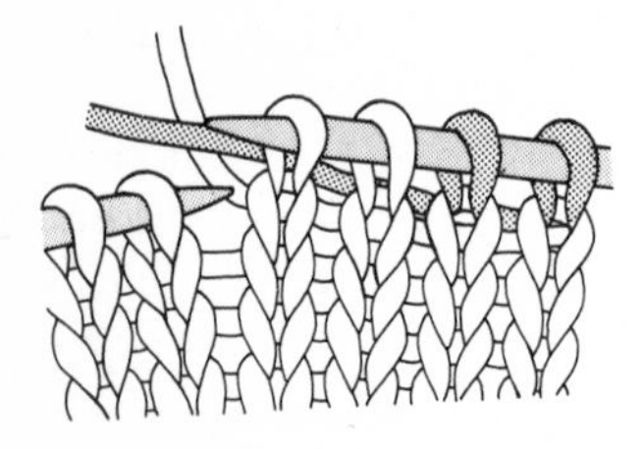

Stranding the yarn at the back of your work

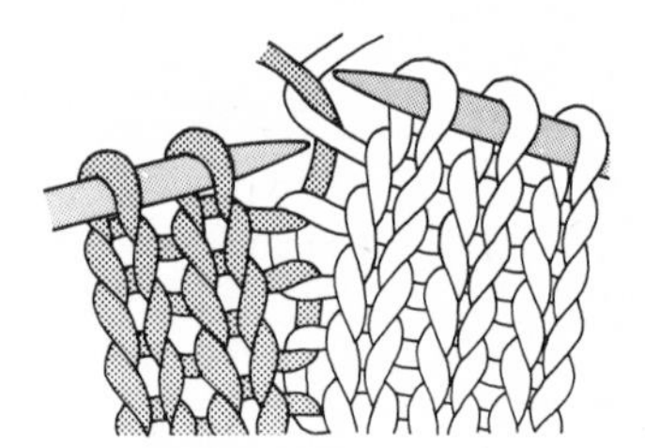

Wrap the old yarn round the new when changing colours

FINISHING A ROW OF MOTIFS

When you have completed a row of motifs cut off the colours you've been using – but not too close to the knitting. On the inside knot together as many ends as you can, using a reef knot which won't come undone. Trim the ends, leaving about an inch of yarn. Any ends you can't knot together should be carefully darned into the knitting so that the darning doesn't show on the right side.

The Patterns

The following patterns were knitted by friends and myself. They are not intended as rigid instructions to be followed exactly – they are examples of what can be made using circular knitting. You will see that we don't specify exact amounts of yarn of a particular brand. This is because we believe that each knitter will want to decide which yarn to use when knitting his/her own designs.

Perhaps at first you'll want to follow the instructions fairly carefully, especially if you've never knitted in tubes before. But once you've knitted a slipover, a skirt or a pair of trousers you'll be introducing variations of your own and inventing your own designs.

Finally, remember that in this kind of knitting 'mistakes' in the pattern don't matter so much: you can use them to give you new ideas for designs and patterns.

So, having mastered the techniques of knitting in fairisle on a circular needle you can begin to knit many exciting, original garments.

1. Slipovers

THIBAUD'S SLIPOVER

I first started inventing my own designs during a holiday on a Czechoslovakian agricultural commune when Pernille caught measles. While Roger and Thibaud explored the farm I sat by her bedside and began to experiment with a circular needle. Since I hadn't brought any patterns with me, I asked Thibaud what he would like. He ordered a slipover with men and galloping horses. His slipover is very simple to make and a good introduction to circular knitting.

MATERIALS

Circular needle size 9; pair of regular needles size 9; crochet hook size 3·50; I used a strand each of Shetland wool and weaving yarn, giving the slipover a distinctive texture, but the choice of yarns is endless (see page 109).

TO KNIT

The following instructions are for a slipover for Thibaud – you'll have to work out how many stitches to cast on for your own version (see page 22).

I first made a paper pattern of the slipover so that I wouldn't have to keep measuring the knitting on Thibaud himself. I then calculated how many stitches to cast on so that the knitting would fit round him – it was 165.

Body

Using the two regular needles cast on 165 stitches and knit them on to the circular needle. Mark the beginning of the round. Having made sure that the stitches are not twisted round the needle, join the knitting.

Knit 6 rows and then knit a row as follows: knit 2 stitches together, make a stitch by bringing the yarn in front of the needle. Continue like this until you have completed the round. This row makes a row of holes which make a notched edge when the first 6 rows are hemmed under.

Now begin to knit in fairisle. I knitted horses, men, etc. For advice on knitting in fairisle see pages 25–8. There are lots of designs at the back of the book to fire your imagination.

Work in fairisle up to the bottom of the armholes – measure this on your paper pattern. Divide the knitting into two equal parts, front and back, leaving the stitches for the back on a spare piece of yarn to stop the knitting unravelling. (You can buy a special stitch-holder for this, or you can use a spare needle with a cork or Sellotape on the end so that the stitches will not come off.)

Front

Knit the front on your circular needle, but knit back and forth rather than round in a tube.

Shape armholes. Cast off 6 stitches at the beginning of the next 2 rows. There is no further shaping for the armhole.

Shape front neckline. You can knit either a square or a V-neck. If you want to make a round neck, see the pattern for Mette's slipover on page 62.

Square neck. Cast off 20 stitches from the middle of the front. The remaining stitches on either side of the V form the straps. Knit each strap separately in garter stitch, measuring the paper pattern to see how long they should be.

V-neck. Find the middle stitch on the front. Knitting each side separately in garter stitch, decrease 1 stitch at the neck edge of each row until there are 10 stitches left. Knit straight to the shoulder.

Shape shoulder (for both square and V-neck). Beginning at the armhole edge of the strap, cast off half the stitches, knit to the end of the row. Knit 1 row and cast off the remaining stitches. Repeat for the other shoulder.

Back

Work the same as the front, but start the neck shaping a little higher.

TO FINISH

Sew the shoulder straps together. Work a row of double crochet round the armholes and neck (see page 106). Turn under and hem the first 6 rows of the body so that the row of holes makes a notched edge.

BABY'S SLIPOVER

This slipover is very easy to make – it could take you just one evening. It will fit a baby of one to two months.

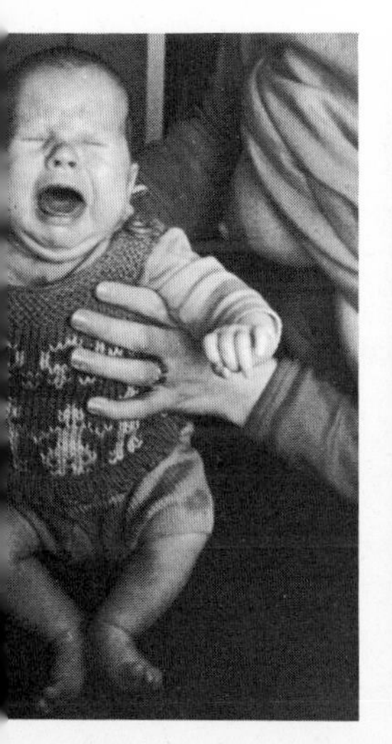

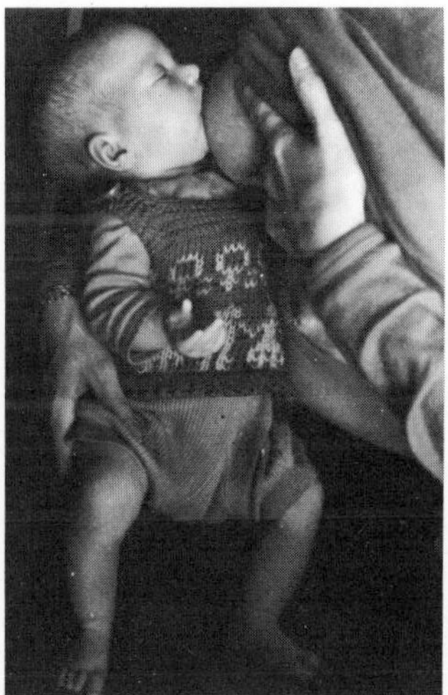

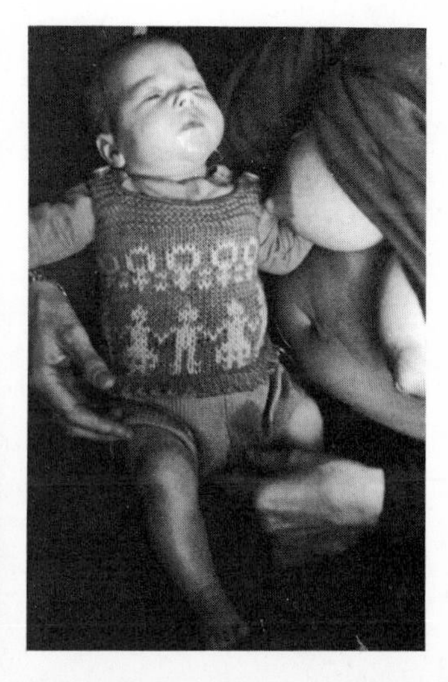

MATERIALS

Circular needle size 9; pair regular needles size 9; crochet hook size 3·50; 4 small buttons; cotton yarn – this will keep the baby cool and not irritate the skin.

TO KNIT

Body

Work out how many stitches you should cast on – a vest for six-week-old Astrid needed 90. Cast the stitches on with the regular needles and knit them on to the circular needle.

Knit 5 rounds. Knit in fairisle for about 6 ins./15 cm.

Divide the stitches into two equal parts, leaving half the stitches, for the back, on a spare piece of yarn. Knit both front and back on your circular needle, knitting back and forth in stocking stitch.

Front bib

Shape armholes. Cast off 4 stitches at the beginning of the next 2 rows. Using your main colour work 8 rows in stocking stitch and cast off.

Back

Shape the armholes as for the front. Using your main colour work 10 rows in stocking stitch.

Shape neckline. Cast off 15 stitches from the middle and knit straps individually with the remaining stitches.

TO FINISH

Work 1 row of single crochet round the neck and armholes (see page 105). Crochet button loops on the straps and sew the buttons to correspond on the bib.

MARTIN'S SLIPOVER

I first met Grete and Martin Rung, who have drawn the illustrations and taken the photographs for this book, through a letter Grete wrote after my first knitting book was published. In it she described how she had knitted a slipover which both she and Martin wear – Martin is wearing it in the photograph.

MATERIALS

Circular needle size 8; circular needle size 10; pair regular needles size 10; set of four double-pointed needles size 10; double knitting yarn.

TO KNIT

Body

First make a paper pattern of the slipover – Grete based hers on an old slipover that fitted well. Knit a swatch and work out how many stitches to cast on.

Cast on the stitches for the bottom using the regular needles and knit them on to the size 10 circular needle. Knit 1 in./2·5 cm in knit 1 purl 1 rib. You can make it larger if you like. (Knitting the ribbing on a finer needle makes the hem more elastic and gives a snug fit round the waist.) Change to the size 8 circular needle and knit in fairisle until you reach the bottom of the armhole. As you can see, Grete knitted flowers, carrots, pears, pigs, and finished with yellow turtles swimming in blue water.

When Grete reached the armholes she was so anxious to wear the garment that she decided to make a slipover rather than a sweater as she'd first intended. So instead of knitting the sleeves, she began to shape the armholes. Divide the knitting into two equal parts. Thread a spare piece of yarn through the stitches for the back to prevent them unravelling. Leave the stitches for the front on the circular needle and for the rest of the garment knit back and forth in stocking stitch.

Front

Shape armholes. Cast off 6 stitches at the beginning of the next 2 rows. Decrease 1 stitch at each end of the next 6 alternate rows – this makes a curved armhole.

Shape neckline. Work without shaping for 4 ins./10 cm. Cast off the middle 10 stitches. Knitting each side of the neckline separately, cast off 1 stitch at the neck edge at the beginning of the next 9 rows. Knit without further shaping until you reach the shoulder on the paper pattern. There should be about 14 stitches left for each shoulder.

Shape shoulder. Cast off 7 stitches at the armhole edge. Knit to the end of the row. Cast off the remaining stitches. Complete the other shoulder to match.

Back

Work as for front but start the shaping for the neckline a little higher.

TO FINISH

Using the set of four double-pointed needles, pick up a stitch from the end of each row round the armholes. Divide the stitches evenly between three of the needles. Work 1 in./2·5 cm in knit 1 purl 1 rib. Finish the neck edge in the same way.

Grete and Martin are such enthusiastic knitters now that they hold knitting parties. Sitting round a pile of balls of wool, they pass the knitting round and let everyone knit as they please. These parties have produced many original sweaters knitted in brilliant patterns – and Grete and Martin have used up their pile of remnants while having a good time. Friends also like recognizing their own knitting in the sweaters.

GRETE'S SLIPOVER

Grete knitted a slipover of the same design as Martin's, but longer and looser and with an abstract pattern.

Using a number 8 circular needle she knitted $1\frac{1}{4}$ ins./3 cm of ribbing to make the hem. Then she began to knit in grey, brown and white – thick homespun yarn and shiny synthetic yarn – using all the remnants she had. Taking the black yarn which she had used for the ribbing, Grete knitted black gnarled trees which wound their way up the changing colours of the background. Using different kinds of yarn gave an interesting texture to the knitting.

There is a fair distance between the trees which would give long threads on the inside, wasting yarn and making large loops, so instead of using one ball of yarn for all the trees, Grete made a small ball for each branch. When she came to each branch she knitted a few stitches from the small ball of yarn.

2. Sweaters and Coats

Now that you've found out how to knit sleeveless slipovers on circular needles, you can add sleeves to make sweaters, jackets and coats. There are three main methods: knitting the body and the sleeves in one piece; knitting sleeves and body separately and setting in the sleeves to complete the garment; knitting the sleeves and body separately up to the armholes and then knitting them together to form a raglan seam.

The following pattern for a baby's sweater is an example of the first method – knitting sleeves and body in one piece.

THE WORLD'S EASIEST BABY SWEATER

Some friends were expecting a baby so I knitted this sweater for them. My mother had found the pattern in a 1930s knitting book. It will fit a 3–6-month-old baby – for a slightly older child knit the sweater on larger needles. The sweater is knitted on regular needles, with 4-ply yarn. If you want to use a different yarn knit a sample first to check how many stitches you will need.

MATERIALS

A pair of regular needles size 11; 4-ply yarn of your choice.

TO KNIT

Cast on 65 stitches and knit 90 rows. To make the sleeves cast on 35 stitches at the beginning of the next 2 rows. Knit 40 rows.

Head opening. Knit 42 stitches. Cast off 51 stitches. Knit the remaining 42 stitches. Next row knit 42 stitches, cast on 51 stitches, knit the remaining 42 stitches.

Knit 40 rows. Cast off 35 stitches at the beginning of the next 2 rows. Knit 90 rows. Cast off.

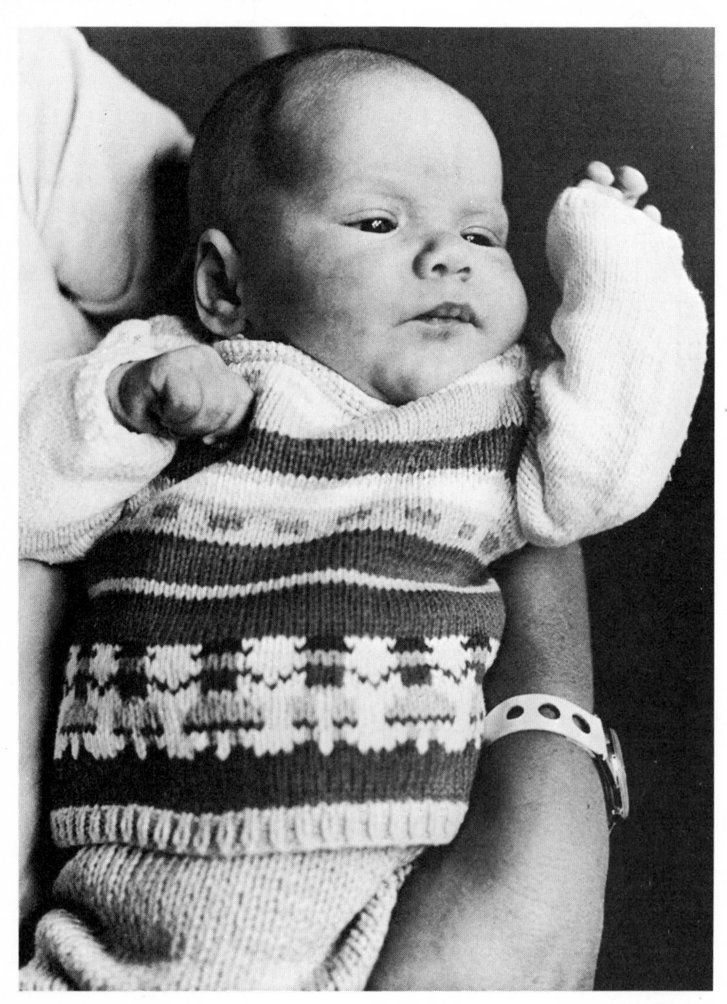

TO FINISH

Sew the side and underarm seams as shown below.

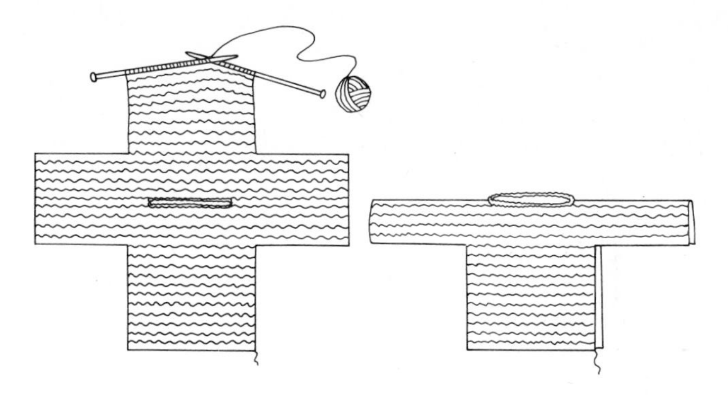

FRUIT AND VEGETABLE PATTERNED SUMMER SWEATER

While standing in front of a grocer's shop one grey January morning and thinking of summer, Charlotte was inspired to make two summer sweaters, patterned with fruit and vegetables.

First of all make a pattern for the fruit and vegetables by x-ing them on squared paper until they look like the real thing (examples are given at the back of the book – pears, grapes, carrots, cherries). You can use up your old remnants of yarn to knit the fruit – either in the natural colours or in less conventional colours.

MATERIALS

Circular needle size 9; set of four double-pointed needles size 9; cotton yarn.

TO KNIT

The body and sleeves are knitted separately; the sleeves are set into the body when the knitting is completed.

Body

First work out how many stitches to cast on. Charlotte is size 36 ins./91 cm; she had to cast on 180 stitches. Work 5 ins./12 cm of knit 2 purl 2 rib, using the background colour. Knit the next round increasing 8 stitches evenly distributed on the round.

Knit 4 rounds and then begin to place the fruit. Charlotte chose seven kinds and knitted a row of each with 4 stitches between each fruit. Between each row of fruit she knitted 4 rounds in the background colour. She placed the pieces of fruit directly over one another as far as possible – this makes it easier to place the motifs. By the time you've knitted the fourth row of fruit you will probably be just under the armholes. Divide the knitting into two equal parts, leaving the stitches for the back on a spare piece of yarn.

Front

Shape armholes. Using the circular needle, but knitting back and forth in stocking stitch, cast off 4 stitches at the beginning of the next 2 rows. Then cast off 2 stitches at the beginning of the next 2 rows. Decrease 1 stitch at each end of every tenth row until you reach the shoulders – there should be about 50 stitches left.

Shape neckline. When you've knitted about 5 ins./12 cm of the front up from the armhole begin to shape the neckline. Cast off the middle 16 stitches. Knit each side of the neckline separately going back and forth in stocking stitch. Decrease 2 stitches at the beginning of the first row on the neck edge. Decrease 1 stitch at the beginning of the next row, work 1 row, decrease 1 stitch at the beginning of the next row. Knit 3 ins./7 cm – or whatever brings you up to the shoulder.

Shape shoulders. Cast off half the remaining stitches, beginning at the armhole edge. Purl 1 row. Cast off the remaining stitches.

Back

Work as for front but begin the neck shaping slightly higher – say 6 ins./15 cm up from the bottom of the armhole.

To finish neckline

Sew the shoulders together. You can either knit a turtle neck or crochet a wide border in double crochet round the neck.

Turtle neck. Start the neck shaping at the front higher up – say 6–7 ins./15–18 cm from the bottom of the armhole. When the front and back are finished, sew the shoulders together. Pick up the stitches from around the neck. Using four needles knit 4 ins./10 cm in knit 2 purl 2 rib in the colour used for the rib border at the hem of the body. Cast off loosely.

Sleeves

Cast on 48 stitches on to four needles. Work 5 ins./12 cm of knit 2 purl 2 rib. On the next round, which is knitted, increase 8 stitches, distributing them evenly through the round. Increase 1 stitch at about the same point on every alternate round until there are about 75 stitches. When the sleeve is as long as you want it up to the base of the armhole cast off 8 stitches above the line of increasings up the arm. Decrease at the top of the sleeves so that they fit into the body armholes. This may involve some trial and error but not very much extra knitting.

TO FINISH

Set in the sleeves to the body.

KIRSTEN'S PEASANT JACKET

The body and sleeves are again knitted separately and the sleeves are set into the body to complete the garment.

MATERIALS

Circular needle, pair of regular needles, set of four double-pointed needles – all the same size; yarn; hooks to fasten the neck opening.

TO KNIT

Body

Knit as for a sleeveless pullover making a notched hem (see page 32). Make it longer and looser so that you can wear other sweaters underneath. The tube should measure about 50 ins./127 cm in circumference.

Knit straight in fairisle until you reach the desired length at the armholes. Divide the knitting into two equal parts and knit the front and back separately. Put the stitches for the back on a spare length of yarn.

Front

Knit back and forth in stocking stitch using the circular needle.

Shape armholes. Cast off 3 stitches at both armhole edges. On the next 3 rows decrease 1 stitch at both ends of the row. Work the armholes without further shaping.

Neck opening. The front is divided into two equal parts at the point where you want to begin the neck opening – measure either from your paper pattern or the person you are knitting for.

Knit in fairisle on the regular needles for about 4 ins./10 cm on both sides of the division. On each purl row knit 2 stitches at the neck opening edge to make a neat border.

Shape neck. Cast off 3 stitches at the neck edge, then work to the end of the row. Work 1 row. Cast off another 3 stitches at the neck edge and work to the end of the row.

Shape shoulders. Cast off half the remaining stitches beginning at the armhole edge. Knit to the end of the row. Work one row. Cast off the remaining stitches.

Back

Knit as for the front, omitting the opening. When the length is the same as the front, shape the neck and shoulders as before.

To finish neck

Sew the shoulders together. Pick up the cast off and decreased stitches round the neckline (but not the front opening) on to the circular needle and knit 5 rows in stocking stitch – don't join the knitting but knit back and forth. Make a row of holes – knit 2 together, make 1, to the end. Work 5 more rows in stocking stitch. Cast off. Turn under the last 5 rows and hem. This makes a notched edge round the neck.

Sleeves

The sleeves are 13 ins./33 cm in circumference. Since this is too small for the smallest circular needle – 16 ins./40·5 cm – you will have to knit the sleeves on four needles.

Knit 5 rounds without any pattern. Make a row of holes – knit 2 together, make 1. Knit to the armhole. You may have to increase a few stitches near the top if you have large upper-arm muscles.

Shape armholes. Cast off 12 stitches. Work the head of the sleeve on the circular needle, knitting back and forth in garter stitch, decreasing 1 stitch at the beginning of each row. Aim to make the top of the sleeve fit the armhole of the body tube. You may not get it right first time but it's quite easy to work out.

TO FINISH

Sew the sleeves into the body.

Sew on hooks at the neck opening as shown in the photograph.

Turn under and hem the first 5 rows on the bottom of the body and sleeves.

SIMPLE SWEATER

It's easy to knit sweaters with set-in sleeves if you make a paper pattern like this:

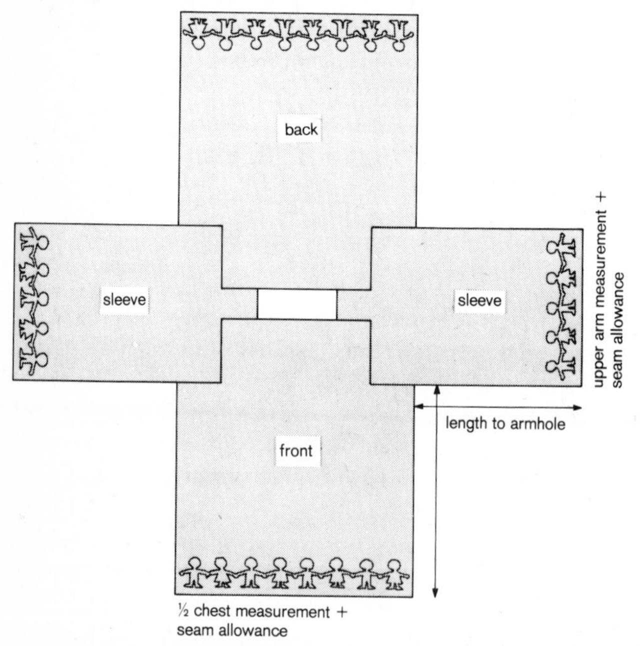

You first of all need to measure the chest, upper arm, length of the body to the armholes, length of the sleeves to the armholes. Draw your pattern using these measurements. Knit a swatch to see how many stitches you knit to the inch/centimetre.

Knit the two body pieces and the two sleeves, on regular needles, the same size as the pattern, shaping the tops of the pieces as shown.

When you've completed the four pieces, sew the sleeves into the body as shown. Finish the neck by crocheting round the edge. Sew the side and underarm sleeve seams.

RAGLAN SEAMING

Attaching sleeves to the body by the raglan method is an easy way of knitting sweaters or jackets with sleeves.

NECESSARY MEASUREMENTS

Chest, wrist, upper arm, circumference of head.

TO KNIT

Knit three tubes. One for the body the circumference of the chest – there is no need to increase or decrease. Work in pattern until you have the length you want at the armhole. Cast off about 10 stitches on both sides of the body.

Knit two tubes for the sleeves, beginning with enough stitches to fit the wrist and gradually increasing to fit the upper-arm measurement. Cast off about 5 stitches at each edge of both sleeves.

Raglan decreasing. Put the body and the sleeves on to a circular needle, matching the cast-off edges of the body with the cast-off edge of each sleeve. Knit round one row, knitting the stitches of the two sleeves and the body. Then decrease 8 stitches every other row – i.e. decrease 2 stitches at the four points where the cast-off edges for the armholes begin and end.

Neckline. Continue to decrease in this way until the remaining stitches on the needle measure the same as the circumference of the head. You can then either cast off or knit a turtle neck (see page 44). To make the neckline more elastic cast off loosely.

TO FINISH

Sew up the underarm seams.

ELSIE'S COTTON SWEATER

In the academic year 1974–5 the students at the Occupational Therapy School decided to exhibit their knitting in Svendborg on the island of Fyn. Among the garments on show was a sweater knitted by Elsie, using the raglan method of attaching sleeves to the body.

MATERIALS

Circular needle size 10; set of four double-pointed needles size 10; cotton yarn.

TO KNIT

Body

Work out how many stitches you need to cast on. Elsie wanted a fairly loose sweater, so cast on 226 stitches. Knit 2 ins./5 cm. Shape the body by increasing 2 stitches on the next row and every following sixth row, 13 times in all. Knit up to the armholes – Elsie knitted 13 ins./33 cm but the length is up to you.

Cast off 12 stitches at each side of the sweater to begin the armholes shaping.

Sleeves

Using the set of four needles, cast on 120 stitches. Knit ¾ in./2 cm, purl 1 row (this makes a neat edge when the first few rows are turned under).

Shape the sleeves by increasing 2 stitches at about the same point on every sixth round 7 times. Increase 2 stitches every eighth round 6 times. Continue to knit in fairisle until the sleeve is the length you want it to the underarm.

Cast off 12 stitches above where the line of increasings is.

Join the sleeves and the body

Knit the body and the sleeves on to the circular needle, so that the cast-off edge of each sleeve is against the cast-off edge of each side of the body. Knit 1 round, thus joining the sleeves to the body.

Shape the raglan. At the four points where the sleeves join the body decrease 2 stitches (i.e. 8 stitches each row) on every other row 23 times. Then in the same way decrease 8 stitches every 4 rows 7 times.

Purl 1 row. Knit $\frac{3}{4}$ in./2 cm. This makes an edge like the one along the hem of the sleeves. Cast off.

TO FINISH

Sew the sweater together at the cast-off edges at the armholes. Turn under and hem the edges round the bottom of the sleeves and around the neck.

THIN COTTON SWEATER WITH SHORT SLEEVES

Elsie made this sweater for herself using the raglan method of joining sleeves to the body.

MATERIALS

Circular needle size 10; set of four double-pointed needles size 10; crochet hook size 2·50; thin cotton yarn.

TO KNIT

Body

To fit chest 34 ins./86 cm, cast on 194 stitches on to the circular needle.

Knit $\frac{3}{4}$ in./2 cm. Make a row of holes – knit 2 together, make 1 all along the row. Knit in fairisle to the armholes and cast off 10 stitches on both sides of the body, to form the armholes.

Sleeves

Using the set of four needles, cast on 56 stitches. Knit $\frac{3}{4}$ in./2 cm followed by a row of holes as on the body. Knit $1\frac{1}{2}$ ins./4 cm. Increase 2 stitches at about the same point on each round 7 times – 14 stitches in all. Cast off 10 stitches above the line of increasings.

Join the sleeves and the body

Put the sleeves and body on the circular needle so that the cast-off edges of the body and the sleeves are together. Knit 1 round.

Shape the raglan. Decrease 8 stitches every fourth row, decreasing 2 stitches at each of the four points where the sleeves and body meet. Decrease in this way 15 times.

On the next round knit a row of holes. Knit 1 round. Cast off.

TO FINISH

Turn up the hems of the sleeves and body. Sew the underarms together. Crochet a string and thread it through the holes at the neck. Fasten the drawstring as you wish.

TO COMBINE CROCHET AND KNITTING

If you prefer crochet to knitting, you might be interested to hear of two ideas from Aase, who comes from the west coast of Jutland.

She knits the body of the sweater up to the armholes, casts off and crochets the upper part of the body; at the same time she attaches the previously crocheted sleeves. Crocheting the sleeves means that there are no long threads on the inside, which can make patterned sweaters easier to put on, especially for children.

Aase also makes colourful and original sweaters by crocheting granny squares which she then crochets together to fit the required chest measurement. She then crochets stripes of colour in rounds above and below the crochet tube. The garment is sewn together and the shoulders and the previously crocheted sleeves sewn into the armholes.

When you've made a few slipovers and sweaters, you'll probably want to try something more ambitious such as a long winter coat.

FULL-LENGTH WINTER COAT

MATERIALS

Circular needle size 8, set of four double-pointed needles size 8; 4-ply natural sheep's wool (the oils in the wool make the coat showerproof), buttons, lining material, such as taffeta quilting, teddy bear fur, or whatever you like.

TO KNIT

Knit three tubes: one for the body, two for the arms. Cast on 250 stitches for the body tube and knit in fairisle to the length required to the shoulders. Before casting off purl 1 row and knit 4 rows. Hem under these 4 rows. Cast on 75 stitches for the sleeves and knit in fairisle to the length required at the armholes.

To make the body opening. Decide where you want to make the opening. Mark this line on the body tube with a long row of running stitches in a yarn which shows up on the pattern. Zigzag on either side of the line of running stitches using a sewing-machine – because you've zigzagged the knitting won't unravel. Pull out the running stitches and cut the knitting carefully straight up between the zigzag lines. Make a border along the cut edge by picking up stitches on the edge from the neckline to the hemline. Knit 6 rows in stocking stitch. Make a row of holes – knit 2 together, make 1. Knit 6 more rows in stocking stitch. Cast off loosely and hem the last 6 rows under.

Armholes. Lap one cut edge of the body over the other as shown in the photographs. Sew the shoulders together. Mark the position of

the armholes with a line of running stitches in a contrasting yarn. The depth of the armholes should measure half the circumference of a sleeve. Using a sewing-machine zigzag on either side of the marked line, curving the stitches slightly at the bottom of the armhole so that they meet. Take out the running stitches and cut the knitting between the two lines of zigzag stitch.

Sew in the sleeves.

Hood

If you want a hood, pick up the stitches around the neck with the circular needle and work back and forth in stocking stitch up to the crown. Cast off and sew the cast-off edge together. The edge of the face opening can be bordered as for the front opening. You can crochet a loop at the base of one side of the hood and sew a tassel to the other, so that the hood fastens at the neck like an Arab burnous.

TO FINISH

I sewed 12 pewter buttons along the flap opening beginning at the shoulder and crocheted corresponding button loops.

You can line your coat. I lined mine with taffeta and a windproof lining, so that it's really warm.

You could also make a belt – I wear my coat Russian-style sometimes with a sash made by my son.

You can make a nice summer cover-up or housecoat knitting the same coat but in a lightweight cotton yarn.

3. Skirts and Dresses

Garments which need a large number of stitches – like skirts and dresses – can easily be knitted on circular needles.

You should line the skirt or dress or wear a slip underneath – the anti-static ones are best – since the wool itches and can be uncomfortable. A lining also helps prevent the skirt from 'seating'.

LONG SKIRT

When I was visiting Lesotholand many people noticed my long patterned skirt. I was contacted by some African women who asked me to show them how I'd made it. I knitted a skirt from locally produced wool and mohair using traditional Lesotho designs.

MATERIALS

Circular needle size 8; wool and mohair yarn; elastic to fit round the waist.

TO KNIT

Work out how many stitches to cast on – the skirt should be wide enough to fit over your hips and allow for easy movement.

Knit 6 rounds. Make a row of holes – knit 2 together, make 1 to the end of the row. Knit 12 rounds, then start to knit in fairisle. I knitted eagles, masks, cottages, and finished with Lesotho's national animal, the crocodile.

At hip height begin to shape the skirt. Every fourth row knit every tenth stitch together with the stitch next to it until you are left with enough stitches to fit round the waist.

Waist casing. When the skirt is the length you want, purl 1 round, knit 6 and cast off loosely.

TO FINISH

Turn under the last 6 rounds, leaving a small gap. Thread the elastic through the waist casing and sew up the gap. Turn under the first 6 rounds at the hem.

When I came home I knitted a long white skirt in the same style, with ladybirds on it.

SAINT HANS EVE SKIRT

Using the same design as my Lesotho skirt, I knitted a skirt to wear on Saint Hans Eve in Denmark. The summer solstice is traditionally a time for celebration in Scandinavia after the long dark winter. Around the twenty-first of June the spirit of winter is dispelled and the crops are blessed. Witches and warlocks are burned in effigy on bonfires to avert pestilence and poverty.

I knitted the skirt with rows of witches, blue lizards, horsetails and spiders. I then bordered the rows of figures with bright wooden beads, gave the animals beady eyes, outlined the figures in gold thread and put bell collars on the lizards. Needless to say, my skirt caused quite a sensation – someone even suggested I try flying on my broomstick!

A KNITTING LETTER FROM TANZANIA

Almost directly under the Southern Cross, five degrees south of the Equator, 1,000 metres above sea level, sit your Danish friends, Jens, Mette, Maj, Lotte and Bodil. They sit looking over Lake Victoria among the banana trees and coffee bushes and knit in colourful patterns. Jens isn't knitting but he and Maj draw pictures for the others.

As far as we know, there's no knitting tradition in this part of the world, though both men and women are involved in other crafts – such as basket-weaving, wood-carving and ceramics.

Jens and Bodil also wrote about the women of Tanzania:

While native Tanzanians are polygamous, the whites are monogamous and discussions of women's status usually centre on this difference. The tendency is for the native Tanzanians to become monogamous since they are heavily influenced by white culture. However, the Tanzanian women outnumber the men by two to one, and because a woman must be married to have appreciable social status or a reasonable way to earn a living – she is a social nonentity if she's unmarried – monogamy causes problems.

In an article 'Polygamy is One Way Out', a journalist suggested a solution to this problem. She exhorted married women not to think of their husbands as private property but to share them with their sisters. They shouldn't just give their husbands permission to take other wives, they should urge them to do so. Their motives could be many: one is that perhaps more wives would support each other against their husbands. At one wedding four wives sang a song for wife number five warning her of their mutual husband's brutality. It was said that with her help they were better able to cope with him.

But hopefully, this endless circle of reasoning can be broken with an understanding of a woman's right to exist independently of a husband.

Warm knitting regards
Jens and Bodil
Bukoba, May 1974

While they were in Tanzania, Bodil and Mette did some knitting. Bodil made a skirt for Lotte and Mette a slipover.

LOTTE'S SKIRT

Bodil began to knit a slipover for her daughter Lotte, but after she had begun she realized she had too many stitches, so rather than begin again, decided to make a skirt.

MATERIALS

Circular needle size 9; cotton yarn; elastic to go round the waist.

TO KNIT

Cast on enough stitches so that the finished skirt will go round your hips comfortably and be wide enough for you to walk easily. For Lotte, who is five years old, Bodil cast on 168 stitches – an adult would need to cast on many more.

Knit 5 rounds. Make a row of holes – knit 2 together, make 1 all along the row. Knit in fairisle until you reach the beginning of the curve of your hip – about 5 ins./12 cm from your waist. Decrease 7 stitches evenly on each round for the next 10 rounds. Knit another 3 ins./7 cm. Make another row of holes. Knit 2 ins./5 cm. Cast off.

TO FINISH

Turn under the first 5 rounds and hem. Turn under the last 2 ins./5 cm to make a casing, leaving a small gap through which to thread the elastic. Thread the elastic through the casing, sew the ends together and sew up the gap.

METTE'S SLIPOVER

Mette had more success with her slipover than Bodil did.

MATERIALS

Circular needle size 9; cotton yarn.

TO KNIT

Body

Mette, who is nine years old, cast on 150 stitches. Knit 5 rounds and then knit a row of holes – knit 2 together, make 1 all along the row. Knit in fairisle for 11 ins./28 cm, or until you reach the armholes.

Divide the knitting into two equal parts and knit the front and back separately, knitting back and forth on the circular needle.

Front

Shape armholes. Cast off 4 stitches at the beginning of the next 2 rows. Decrease 1 stitch at the beginning of each row for the next $1\frac{1}{4}$ ins./3 cm.

Shape neck. Cast off the middle 18 stitches. To make the neckline slightly rounded, cast off 1 stitch at the neck edge for the next 6 rows.

Knit shoulder straps with the remaining stitches on either side of the neck until they reach the shoulder. Cast off.

Back

Work the same as the front, but start the neck shaping a little higher.

TO FINISH

Turn under the first 5 rounds and hem. Sew the shoulder straps together.

CHILD'S DRESS

If you make a long slipover, you have a dress which can become a slipover when the child grows. This dress was knitted for a three-year-old – if you want a larger dress, cast on more stitches at the hem.

MATERIALS

Circular needle size 9; regular needles size 9; crochet hook size 2·50; double knitting yarn.

TO KNIT

Body

Cast on 160 stitches using the regular needles and knit them on to the circular needle. Knit 6 rounds. Make a row of holes – knit 2 together, make 1 to the end of the row. Knit in fairisle as far as the armholes.

Divide the knitting into two equal parts, putting the stitches for the back on a spare piece of yarn. Work the front on the circular needle, but knit back and forth in stocking stitch.

Front

Shape armholes. Cast off 5 stitches at the beginning of the next 2 rows. Work 2 ins./5 cm in stocking stitch, decreasing 1 stitch at both ends of each row.

Shape neckline. Cast off the middle 2 stitches. Knit each side of the neck separately. Decrease 1 stitch at the neck edge of every row until each side measures about 3 ins./7 cm.

Shape shoulders. Cast off half the remaining stitches beginning at the armhole edge. Work to the end of the row. Work 1 row. Cast off the remaining stitches.

Back

Work as for the front.

TO FINISH

Turn under the first 6 rounds and hem. Sew the shoulders together. Crochet 1 row of double crochet around the neck and armholes.

TREE OF LIFE DRESS

During one long winter I knitted a long dress based on an extended slipover.

The dress was patterned with a design based on the tree of life in Nordic mythology – Yggdrasil. As the tree grew I populated it with birds, butterflies, animals and flowers. In the middle of the stomach a woman's face peers out from behind the foliage. A peacock's tail fans out across the back just where I decreased sharply for the waist.

I knitted the dress in 3-ply Shetland yarn and mohair, but I also used all kinds of remnants of different plys and colours that I thought went well with the dark purple and green shades of the tree.

4. Trousers and Playsuits

Knitting trousers on circular needles is very easy – there are no seams to sew and the nylon wire holds the long length of knitting without strain. When you've discovered how to knit trousers, you can combine them with slipovers to make playsuits and bathing suits.

TROUSERS

Dear Sister,

Measure yourself at the thickest point of your thigh. Using the yarn and circular needle of your choice, cast on enough stitches to cover that circumference.

Knit 9 rounds, purl 1 round. Continue to knit in fairisle until the leg measures about 4 ins./10 cm from where the crotch will be.

Now begin to knit and purl back and forth on your circular needle until you reach the crotch. Put the stitches for the first leg on a spare piece of yarn.

Knit the second leg as the first.

Put both legs on to the circular needle, with the crotch edges together. Between the legs, back and front, cast on 5–10 stitches for the gusset. Then decrease on each side of the gusset on every second row until none of these cast-on stitches remain. This gives a triangular shape on either side of the crotch to allow room for movement.

Knit up to the waistline. Purl 1 round, knit 9 rounds. Cast off.

Hem the legs so that the purl row forms a neat edge. Sew the crotch together. Turn under the 9 rounds at the waist and insert elastic.

Love Ninon.

PLAYSUIT FOR A TWO- TO THREE-YEAR-OLD

I knitted this suit for my daughter Pernille. The following summer I added crochet ruffles on the legs. By also knitting a pair of long socks I was able to compensate for the amount Pernille had grown during the winter. But the summer after we finally had to give the playsuit to a cousin, who is also called Pernille.

MATERIALS

Circular needle size 10; regular knitting needles size 10; set of four double-pointed needles size 10; cotton yarn; 2 buttons.

TO KNIT

First leg

Cast on 100 stitches on to the four needles and knit 5 rounds. Purl 1 round. Decrease 4 stitches on the next round, distributing them evenly on the round. Decrease in the same way on the next 3 rounds.

Knit until you are 2 ins./5 cm from the crotch. Increase 4 stitches on the next round, distributing them evenly. Increase in the same way on the next round. Cast on enough stitches to fit the crotch.

Crotch. The crotch is knitted and purled back and forth on the circular needle or knitted on regular needles in stocking stitch.

Cast off 3 stitches at the beginning of the next 2 rows. Cast off 2 stitches at the beginning of the next 2 rows. Decrease 1 stitch at the beginning of the next row; increase 1 stitch in the middle of the row; decrease 1 stitch at the end. Work one more row in the same way. Transfer knitting to a piece of spare yarn.

Second leg

Knit as for the first leg with the crotch on the opposite side so that the pattern will match.

Body

Put both legs on to the circular needle, making sure that the crotch edges are together. Knit in fairisle as far as the armholes. Divide the knitting into two equal parts. Knit the back and front separately, knitting back and forth in stocking stitch on the circular needle.

Front

On the next row knit 2 together 3 times at both ends of the row. Knit 2 together twice at each end of the next 2 rows. On the next 3 rows knit 2 together once at each end of the row.

Knit 10 rows without decreasing.

Next row: cast off the middle 17 stitches.

Straps. Knit the two straps separately. Decrease 3 stitches evenly on the first row; on the second row decrease 2 stitches evenly; on the third and fourth rows decrease 1 stitch in the centre of the row.

Knit without decreasing until the straps reach the shoulders. (The straps should overlap each other for buttoning.)

Buttonholes. 5 rows from the end work 1 buttonhole on each strap. Cast off the 2 middle stitches. On the next row cast on 2 stitches where the middle stitches were cast off. Knit a few more rows and cast off.

Back

Work as for the front, omitting the buttonholes on the straps.

TO FINISH

Sew the crotch together and sew on the buttons to correspond with the buttonholes. Turn under and hem the first 5 rounds at the bottom of the legs.

BATHING SUIT

You can see Martin in the photograph with his older brother – who is wearing a swim-suit knitted by his wife. Martin knitted his own swim-suit. He wanted a sea theme and so chose to knit green seaweed, blue water and goldfish, and finished with a four-pointed North Star.

MATERIALS

Circular needle size 9; 2 buttons; cotton yarn.

TO KNIT

Pants

These are knitted from the waist down. Cast on 110 stitches and knit 20 rounds. Or adjust these figures according to your dimensions and tension. Increase 2 stitches at two points on either side of the back for about 15 rounds. This makes some extra space for the backside. Knit 20 rounds without shaping.

Gusset

From the middle of the front and back knit 20 stitches for about 20 rows, knitting backwards and forwards in stocking stitch. Leave the other stitches on a spare piece of yarn.

Sew these strips together to make the gusset.

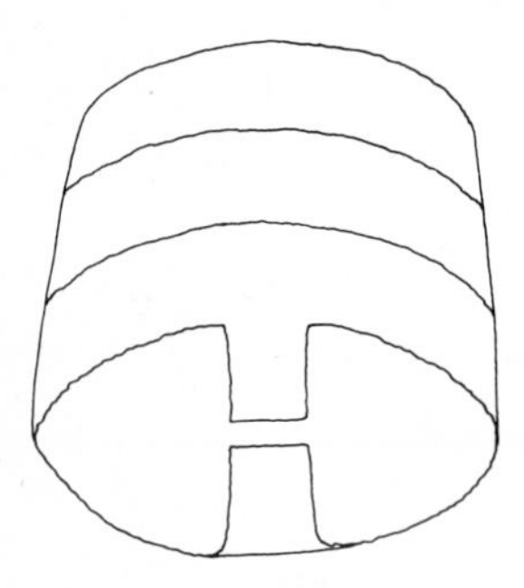

Legs

Pick up stitches along one side of the gusset and knit the legs down the middle of your thigh. End with 1 in./2·5 cm of knit 2 purl 2 ribbing to form the hem. Knit the other leg in the same way. You now have a pair of pants.

Top

Pick up the first round of stitches on the pants on your circular needle and knit 30 rounds. Cast off one third of the stitches at the back. Continue with the remaining stitches to make the bib.

Bib. Knitting back and forth in stocking stitch on the circular needle, decrease 1 stitch at the beginning of each row for 10 rows. Knit in fairisle until you want to start knitting the straps – you can either have a high or low bib with correspondingly short or long straps.

Cast off the middle stitches of the bib, leaving 15 at each end for the straps.

Straps. Work the straps in stocking stitch until they are long enough to reach the top back of the pants where they will button. Five rows before the end make a buttonhole on each strap – if you don't know how to make buttonholes, see the instructions for the child's playsuit (see page 68). Cast off.

TO FINISH

Sew the buttons on the back of the suit at the top of the pants.

5. Ponchoes

Ponchoes are very useful on cold days. You can either wear them over indoor clothes or for extra warmth over a coat. You have to cast on a lot of stitches, but a large circular needle holds them comfortably, and once you start knitting in fairisle the work grows very quickly.

POINTED PONCHO

MATERIALS

Circular needle size 9; Icelandic mountain sheep's wool (pages 115–16).

TO KNIT

Cast on 360 stitches and knit $\frac{3}{4}$ in./2 cm.

Shape as follows: at the beginning of the next round knit 2 together, knit 2, knit 2 together. Knit to a point half-way round the work and repeat. Continue to decrease in this way every other row at the same points on the front and back.

Continue knitting until the poncho is the desired length. Decrease several stitches evenly on the next few rounds until 64 stitches remain. Knit 1 round, purl 1 round for the collar. Cast off.

ROUND PONCHO

MATERIALS

Circular needle size 10; 4-ply yarn.

TO KNIT

Cast on 435 stitches. Knit 10 rounds. Make a round of holes – knit 2 together, make 1 to end. Knit 12 rounds.

Now begin to knit in fairisle. Decrease 15–20 stitches evenly every seventh or tenth round – this means you have 7–10 rounds in which to knit a fairisle pattern without being hampered by decreasing.

When the poncho measures 24 ins./61 cm from the row of holes decrease as above, but with only 4–5 rounds between the decreasing rounds. When the poncho measures 29 ins./74 cm from the row of holes finish decreasing and work 4½ ins./11 cm in knit 1 purl 1 rib. Cast off.

6. Hats

Knitting hats is a good way of learning to use a set of four needles – and you can knit a hat in an evening. They are also, of course, very warm to wear in winter.

HAT WITH A POINTED CROWN

Dudi is fifteen. She loves riding and wanted a hat with horses on. Here are the instructions for the hat she knitted.

MATERIALS

Set of four double-pointed needles size 8; pair of regular needles size 8; Icelandic mountain sheep's wool (see pages 115–16).

TO KNIT

Cast on 85 stitches with the four needles and knit in fairisle for 5 ins./12 cm. When Dudi had knitted a few rows of her pattern she discovered she had no room for the front half of the last horse, so she knitted a tree in the middle of the horse so that it looked as if the animal was hiding behind it.

Shape the crown. Knit 2 together every 6th or 7th stitch. Knit 2 rounds without decreasing. Repeat these 3 rounds until there are only 3 or 4 stitches. Cast off.

Earflaps (optional, for extra warmth)

Check where your ears are in relation to the hat. At these two points pick up 20 stitches from the first round of the hat. Using regular needles, work 6 rows of stocking stitch. Knit 2 together at the beginning of each row until no more stitches remain.

TO FINISH

Double crochet 1 row round the edges of the earflaps and hat. Crochet two strings and attach them to the points of the earflaps.

HAT WITH A ROUNDED CROWN

Work as for the pointed hat until you reach the decreasing on the crown.

Shape as follows: knit 2 together, knit 5 – repeat these 7 stitches to the end of the round. Work 1 round without decreasing. Repeat these 2 rounds until 3–4 stitches remain. Cast off.

You can add earflaps to this hat as well.

7. Gloves and Mittens

Like hats, gloves and mittens are knitted on sets of four double-pointed needles. The idea of knitting fingers and thumbs may make you feel all thumbs at first, but with practice gloves and mittens are very quick and easy to knit.

Before you start, a few points to remember:

Remember that knitting in fairisle makes the work slightly tighter. It is therefore a good idea to knit in fairisle on the wrist and hand rather than on the fingers where the pattern would be confused and your fingers would get caught in the connecting strands of yarn.

Decreasing at the thumb is the same for both sides – this makes the left- and right-hand gloves or mittens interchangeable.

If you want a tight wrist, you can knit 2 ins./5 cm of ribbing at the start of the gloves or mittens.

GLOVES

MATERIALS

Set of four double-pointed needles size 8; thin mohair yarn – this combination of needles and yarn makes the fabric of the gloves very elastic so that they will fit most adult hands.

TO KNIT

When you're following these instructions you may find it helpful to also follow the diagram – this will help you understand how the gloves

are knitted, and thus make it easier for you to invent your own pattern.
Cast on 45 stitches. Work 23 rounds in fairisle.

Thumb. Increase 1 stitch, knit 5 stitches for the thumb, increase 1 stitch. Knit the rest of the round. Knit 2 more rounds, increasing 1 stitch at each of the points where you increased on the first round.

Here the hand gets wider so increase 10 stitches on the next round, distributing them evenly on the round, but excluding the stitches for the thumb.

Knit 3 more rounds, increasing 2 stitches at the thumb as before. There are now 17 stitches for the thumb. Put these stitches on to a safety pin – you knit the thumb when the rest of the glove is complete.

Knit 10 rounds with the stitches for the hand. Flatten the knitting on a table so that the root of the thumb is folded exactly down the middle and the thumb lies exactly on one side of the knitting. Now you are ready to knit the fingers.

Index finger

(This is of course on the side nearest the thumb.) Put 5 stitches from one side and 6 from the other side on to the needles. Put all the other stitches on a spare piece of yarn. Increase 1 stitch between the index finger and the point where the middle finger will go. There are now 12 stitches. Knit 17 rounds and cast off by knitting 2 stitches together until no more stitches remain.

Middle finger

Put the next 8 stitches from one side and the next 7 from the other side on to your needles. Increase 1 stitch in the space between the middle finger and where the ring finger will go. There are now 16 stitches. Knit 20 rounds and cast off as for the index finger.

Ring finger

Put the next 6 stitches from one side and the next 7 stitches from the other side on to your needles. Increase 1 stitch between the ring

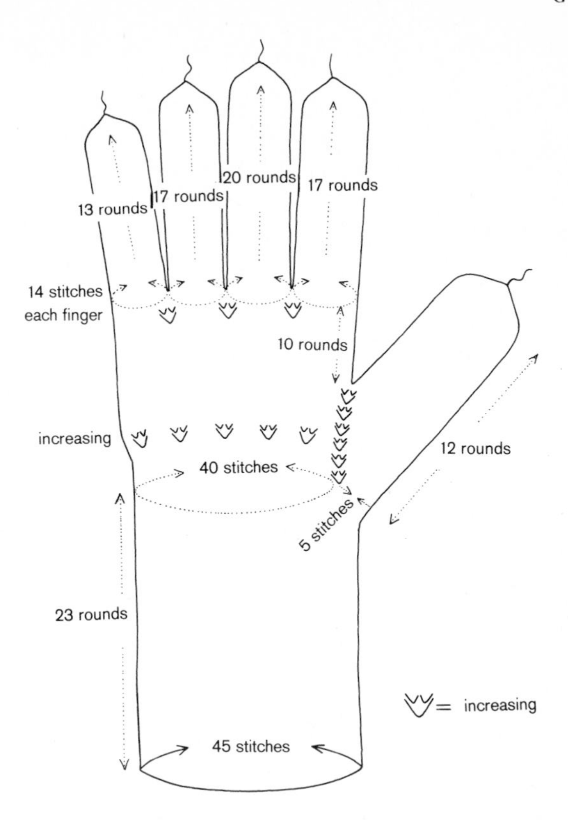

finger and where the little finger will be. There are now 14 stitches. Knit 17 rounds and cast off as for the index finger.

Little finger

Put the last 14 stitches on to your needles. Knit 13 rows and cast off as for the index finger.

Thumb

Put the 17 stitches for the thumb on to your needles and knit enough rounds to almost cover the thumb. Cast off as for the index finger.

Grete's gloves were so successful that her father asked her to knit a pair for him. He wanted his hands to look like a bunch of carrots. The hands were deep green and the fingers orange. Grete even crocheted strings on to the finger tips to look like roots. Her father looks wonderful on the train going to work as he holds up his newspaper with his carrot fingers. Some of the passengers glance at his hands and then look out of the window. One morning a young man sitting opposite suddenly said, 'My friend Charlotte sends her regards.' Puzzled, Grete's father asked how the man knew who he was. 'Oh, when I saw those gloves I knew you had to be Grete's father.'

MITTENS

MATERIALS

Set of four double-pointed needles; yarn of your choice.

TO KNIT

First of all measure your wrist and work out how many stitches you should cast on.

Knit in fairisle until you reach the base of the thumb. Put the next 10 stitches on to a safety pin and cast on 10 extra stitches. Knit the rest of the round.

Continue knitting in fairisle until you reach a point 3 ins./7 cm below the tip of your middle finger.

Shaping. Flatten the mitten on a table, making sure that the hole for the thumb is folded exactly in half. Mark where the knitting is folded on both sides with a piece of contrasting yarn. Carry on knitting round but knit 2 stitches together at the two points marked until the knitting just covers your hand. Cast off the remaining stitches.

Thumb

Pick up the 10 stitches you cast on at the thumb and put them, together with the 10 stitches from the safety pin, on to the needles. Knit round on these 20 stitches until the mitten's thumb is nearly as long as yours. Cast off as for the index finger in the gloves pattern (see page 78).

8. Socks

Good thick socks to wear with clogs or inside winter boots are very expensive to buy. It's much cheaper – and more enjoyable – to knit your own.

Before you begin knitting, some advice from an expert sock knitter:

Pure wool is nice to knit with and the finished socks look very good, but you risk wearing holes in the toes and heels after the first week of wear. For strength and durability socks should be knitted with a blend of nylon and wool – say 80 per cent wool and 20 per cent nylon.

Be very careful when you knit in fairisle on the sock foot since the knitting tends to tighten. The socks are then difficult to put on and you can catch your toes in the linking strands. If you're a beginner, it's best to knit patterns on the legs only – in any case no one can see much of your sock foot when you're wearing shoes.

HOW TO KNIT SOCKS

These socks were knitted for a three-year-old child. If you want to knit larger socks, increase the number of stitches you cast on so that they fit round the leg and foot.

MATERIALS

Set of four double-pointed needles size 9; 4-ply yarn in mixture of wool and nylon. (These needles and yarn produce fairly thin socks; for thicker socks use thicker needles and yarn and adjust the number of stitches.)

TO KNIT

Leg. Cast on 42 stitches for the top of the sock. Knit in fairisle until the leg is the desired length from the ankle.

Heel. Knit this with doubled yarn of one colour to make it stronger. Leave 20 stitches on one needle. Knit a gusset for the heel on these stitches alone by decreasing 1 stitch at both ends of each row until 9 stitches remain. Then increase 1 stitch at both ends of every row until you have 20 stitches again. The heel is sewn together when the sock is completed. Put the 42 stitches on to the needles again.

Foot. Knit the foot straight until you reach the tip of the little toe. The toe can be knitted with doubled yarn to make it stronger. Beginning at the little-toe side decrease as follows: knit 2 together, knit 2, knit 2 together, knit to the end of the round. Continue decreasing like this until you get to the point where the big toe begins to curve. Now decrease as for the little toe on the big-toe side, while continuing to decrease on the other side for the little toe. Decrease on the big-toe side six times.

Cast off the remaining stitches.

TO FINISH

Sew the heel together. Sew the cast-off edge together at the toes.

You can make slippers from these socks by sewing a piece of leather the shape of your foot on to the sole.

EMANCIPATED TOES

Once you've knitted gloves with fingers, you can knit socks with toes.

Knit the sock as normal until you get to the toe shaping. Put the sock on and work out the size of your 'toe holes'. Then simply knit toes as you knit fingers in gloves (see the gloves pattern on page 77). Try knitting each toe in a different colour.

9. Cushion Covers

SCATTER CUSHION COVERS

My cushions had begun to look dull so I decided to knit brightly patterned covers for them.

MATERIALS

Circular needle size 9; cotton yarn.

TO KNIT

Measure the cushion, knit a swatch and work out how many stitches to cast on. The cushion will look better if the cover is slightly tight.

Cast on the stitches and knit in fairisle until you've enough knitting to fit the pad. Cast off by folding the circular needle together and knitting the stitches off two at a time (one from each side of the circular needle) on to a regular needle. Then cast off.

TO FINISH

Sew a zipper into the open end so that the cover can be removed for washing.

SWEDISH BENCH COVER

To match my scatter cushions I decided to knit a cover for my Swedish bench.

MATERIALS

Circular needle size 9; cotton yarn – again make the cover slightly tight so that it will not bunch.

TO KNIT

Work out how many stitches to cast on to fit the bench. Cast them on and knit in fairisle until the work fits the bench. Cast off as for the cushion cover and sew in a zip.

I knitted my cover while travelling each day from my home in Espergærde to Copenhagen – the other passengers were amazed at the mass of knitting in my bag.

10. Children Knitting

If you're a beginner at knitting, it's easier to start with something small – such as the clothes for a doll or a teddy bear on the next three pages. In knitting clothes for toys you can also practise techniques like increasing, decreasing, casting off and on. Experienced knitters can of course knit clothes for themselves and their friends, using this book as inspiration.

If you are a beginner, here are some points to remember:

Since the shortest circular needle is 16 ins./40·5 cm long, clothes for toys have to be knitted on sets of four double-pointed needles. For guidance on this see page 19.

When you knit in fairisle, remember to start reading the chart from the bottom right and knit your pattern from right to left.

Try to fit your pattern to the number of stitches you have but don't worry too much if you must end a round with only part of a motif – the knitting will look fine anyhow.

If the strands on the wrong side get too long, interweave them now and again (see page 27).

When you knit with several colours, keep the balls on the inside so that they won't tangle.

If you make a mistake try to correct it on the following round instead of undoing all the stitches. It's not much fun to have to correct mistakes all the time so just continue knitting – small mistakes are hardly noticeable.

You will of course need to work out how many stitches to cast on. See page 22 for instructions on how to do this.

If you would like to make a doll to knit clothes for, there's a pattern and instructions for making one on page 94.

DOLL'S LONG DRESS

MATERIALS

Set of four double-pointed needles; pair of regular needles; yarn of your choice.

TO KNIT

First of all work out how many stitches you should cast on to go round the doll's waist. Cast on double that number. Knit 10 rounds before you start knitting in fairisle. Then knit in fairisle as far as the arm-holes – put the knitting on the doll to see where this should be.

Knit the next round as follows: alternately knit 2 stitches, then knit 2 together. Knit 1 round. Repeat the decreasing round once more. You now have the correct number of stitches to fit the waist.

Put the stitches for the back on to a spare piece of yarn to stop them unravelling. Knit the back and front separately on a pair of regular needles the same size as the four needles.

Front

Using the stitches for the front knit 10 rows. Count the stitches and cast off the middle third.

Straps. Knit one shoulder strap until it comes up to the shoulder. Knit the other strap the same.

Back

Knit as for the front.

TO FINISH

Turn under and hem the first $\frac{1}{2}$ in./1 cm on the knitting. If the dress is for a rag doll sew the shoulder straps together. If it's for a plastic doll, sew press-studs on to the straps.

LONG TROUSERS WITH BRACES FOR A DOLL

MATERIALS

Set of four double-pointed needles; regular needles; yarn of your choice.

TO KNIT

Knit the skirt of the long dress as on page 89. Cast off.

Turn the knitting inside out. Mark the centre back with a line of running stitches, sewing through both the front and back of the dress.

Measure the knitting on the doll and mark where the crotch is. Using a sewing machine, zigzag on either side of the marked line, curving the zigzags at the crotch so that they meet. Take out the running stitches and cut between the two lines of zigzags. Hem the two seams.

Turn the trousers inside out and slip them on your doll. Attach braces to keep the trousers up – pieces of coloured elastic look very authentic.

DOLL'S SHORT DRESS

MATERIALS

Set of four double-pointed needles; pair of regular needles; yarn of your choice.

TO KNIT

Work out how many stitches you need to fit round the doll's waist. Cast on that number, plus half again.

Knit in fairisle until the knitting reaches from the doll's knees to the waist.

Divide the knitting into two equal parts and put the stitches for the back on to a spare piece of yarn. Knit the back and front separately on regular needles.

Front

Knit 2 stitches together at the beginning of each row until you are left with half the number of stitches you had when you started knitting the front.

Straps. Divide the remaining front stitches in half and work one strap in stocking stitch until it reaches the shoulder. Cast off. Knit the second strap in the same way.

Back

Knit the back like the front.

TO FINISH

Either sew press-studs on the straps or sew them together.

BABY'S SLIPOVER

If you've just had a new brother or sister – or know someone who has – why don't you knit a baby's slipover?

MATERIALS

Set of four double-pointed needles size 9; pair of regular needles size 9; yarn of your choice.

TO KNIT

Body

Cast on 100 stitches. Knit 10 rounds before you start knitting in fairisle.

Knit in fairisle for about 7 ins./18 cm, until you reach the armholes. Cast off 5 stitches on opposite sides of the knitting. Leave half the stitches on a spare piece of yarn.

Front

Knit the front with the remaining stitches using the regular needles. Knit 12 rows.

Straps. Knit 15 stitches. Cast off 15. Knit 12 rows on the remaining 15 stitches. Cast off. Knit the other strap using the first 15 stitches.

Back

Knit as for the front.

TO FINISH

If you know how, double crochet an edge round the neck and armholes, but it's not really necessary.

Sew press-studs on to the shoulder straps.

Hem under $\frac{3}{4}$ in./2 cm round the bottom of the slipover.

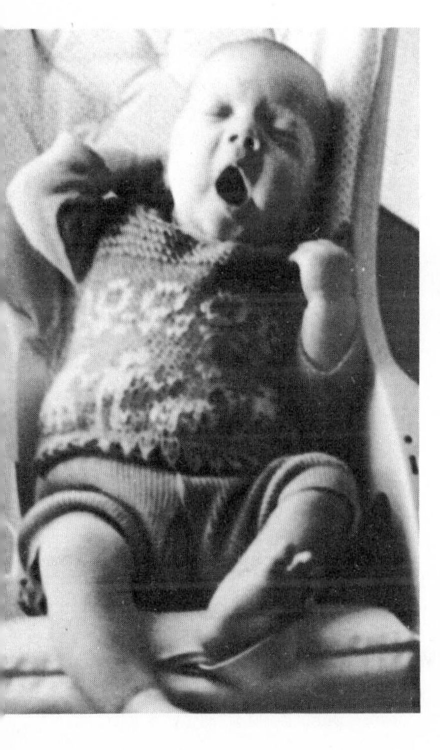

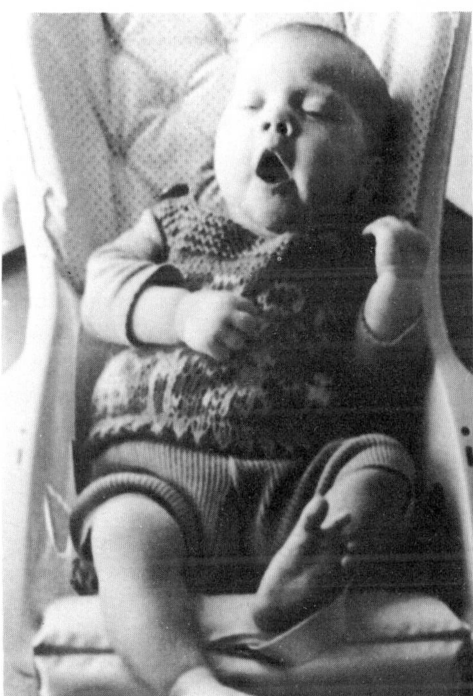

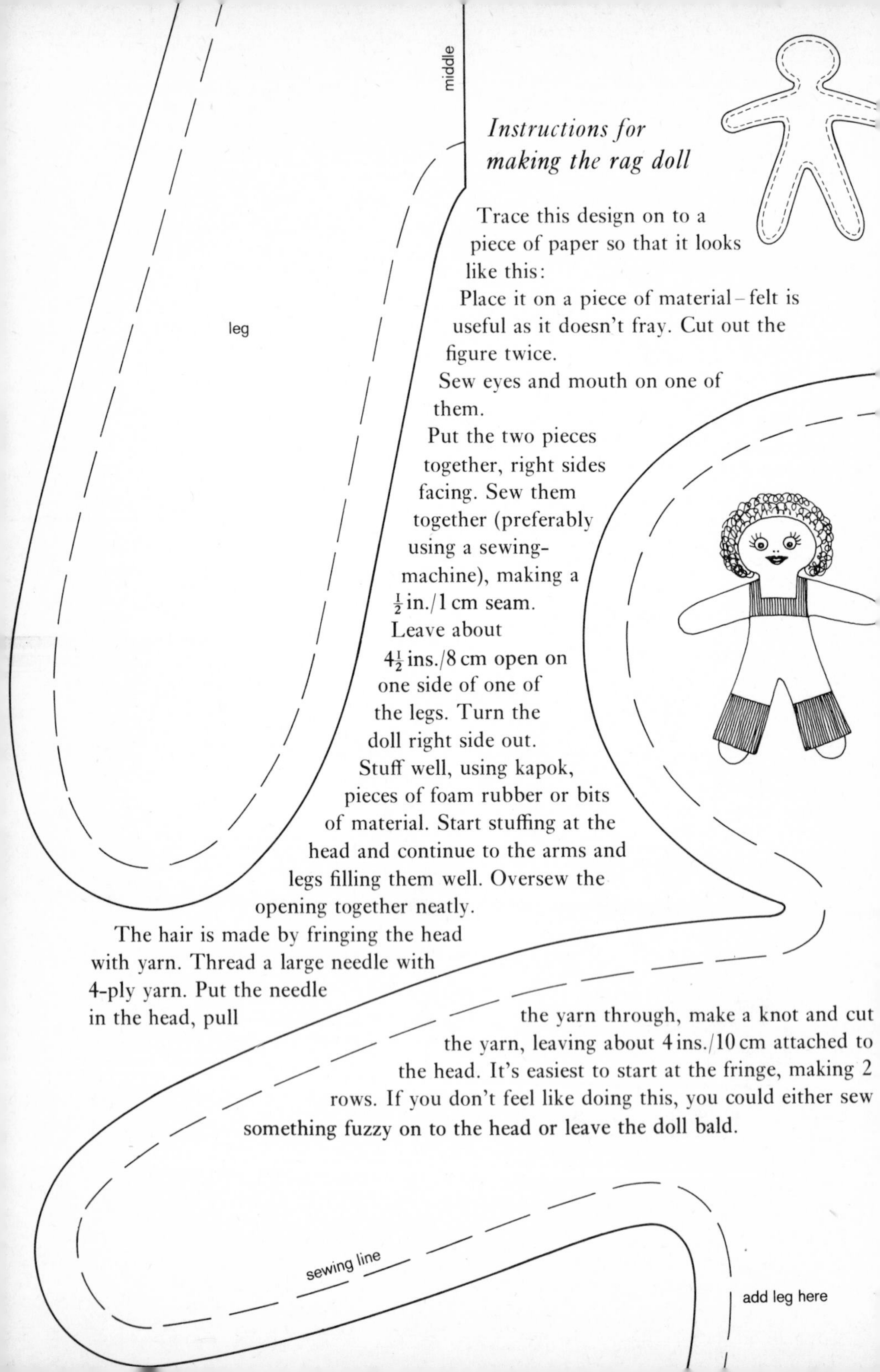

Instructions for making the rag doll

Trace this design on to a piece of paper so that it looks like this:

Place it on a piece of material – felt is useful as it doesn't fray. Cut out the figure twice.

Sew eyes and mouth on one of them.

Put the two pieces together, right sides facing. Sew them together (preferably using a sewing-machine), making a ½ in./1 cm seam.

Leave about 4½ ins./8 cm open on one side of one of the legs. Turn the doll right side out.

Stuff well, using kapok, pieces of foam rubber or bits of material. Start stuffing at the head and continue to the arms and legs filling them well. Oversew the opening together neatly.

The hair is made by fringing the head with yarn. Thread a large needle with 4-ply yarn. Put the needle in the head, pull the yarn through, make a knot and cut the yarn, leaving about 4 ins./10 cm attached to the head. It's easiest to start at the fringe, making 2 rows. If you don't feel like doing this, you could either sew something fuzzy on to the head or leave the doll bald.

Learning to Knit

TO CAST ON

1. Have a seat. A comfortable one.

2. Take the yarn and two straight needles.

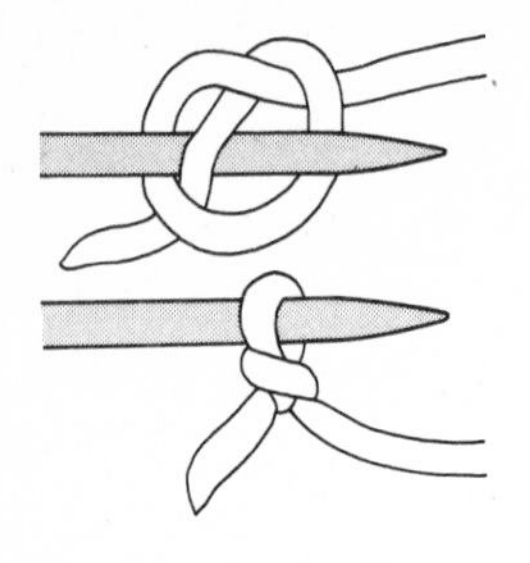

3. Make a slip knot and put it on the left-hand needle.

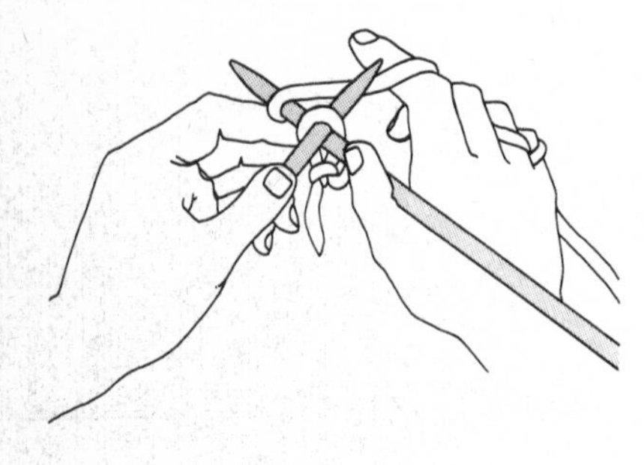

4. Insert the right-hand needle into the loop from front to back, and wind the yarn round the point of the needle.

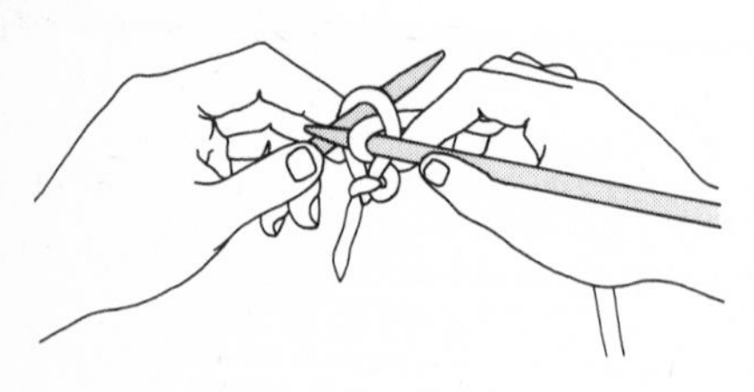

5. Pull the new loop through the first one and slip it on to the left-hand needle.

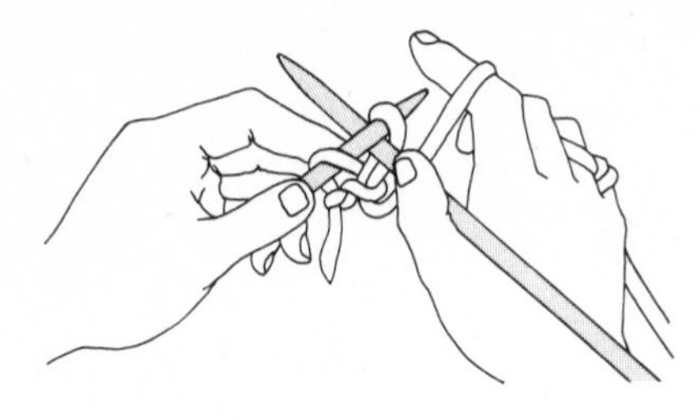

6. Insert the point of the right-hand needle between the first and second loops, wind the yarn round the needle and pull the new stitch through. Then slip it on to the left-hand needle, and make the next stitch by inserting the needle between the last two loops.

This is only one of several different methods of casting on; more experienced knitters may prefer to cast on by their usual method.

TO KNIT

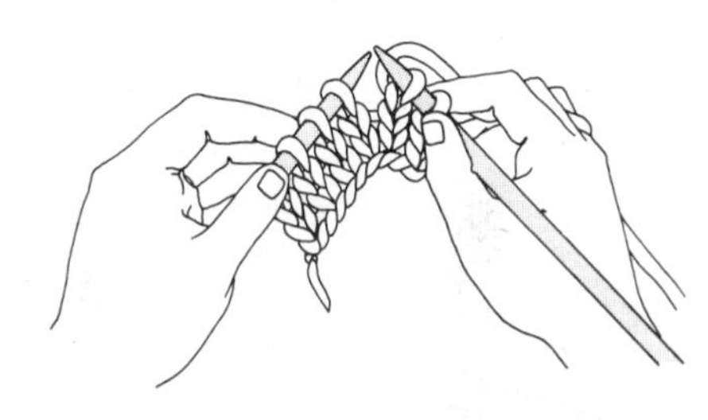

1. Hold the needles like this.

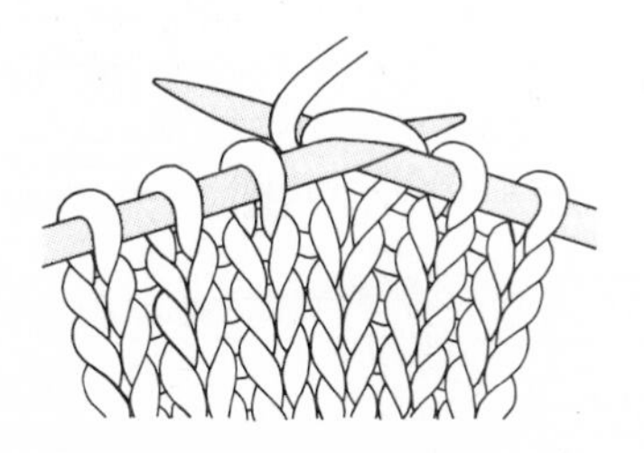

2. Put the point of the right-hand needle through the first stitch on the left-hand needle from front to back. Keeping the yarn at the back, wind it round the point of the right-hand needle.

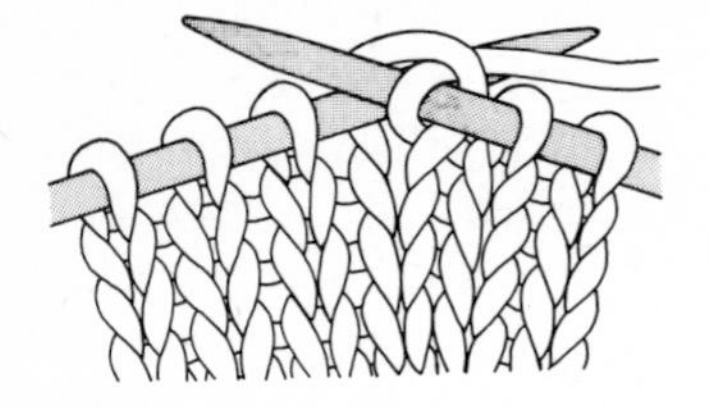

3. Pull the new loop through the stitch on the left-hand needle and let the stitch on the left-hand needle slip off.

TO PURL

Hold the needles when you begin the same as when you start to do the knit stitch.

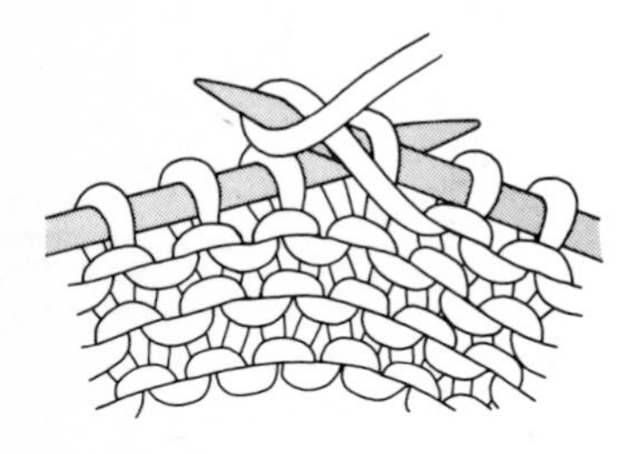

1. Put the point of the right-hand needle through the first stitch on the left-hand needle from back to front. Keep the yarn at the front of the work. Put it round the top of the right-hand needle.

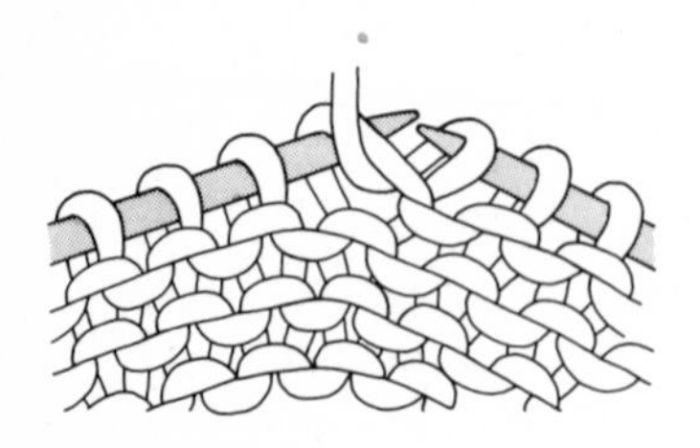

2. Draw the loop you've made through the stitch on the right-hand needle. Keep this new stitch on the right-hand needle and let the stitch on the left-hand needle slip off.

TO CAST OFF

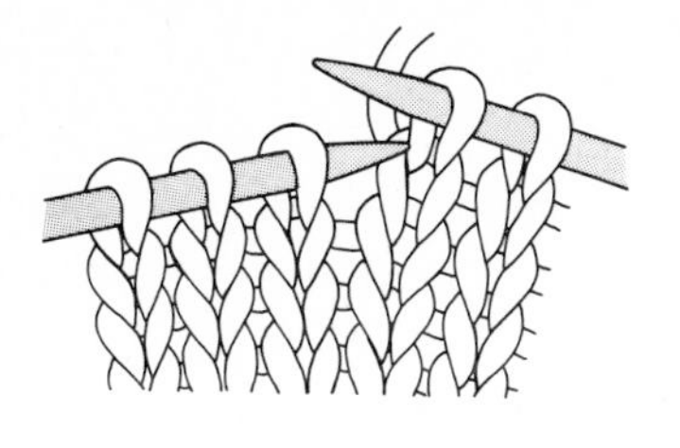

1. Knit two stitches LOOSELY

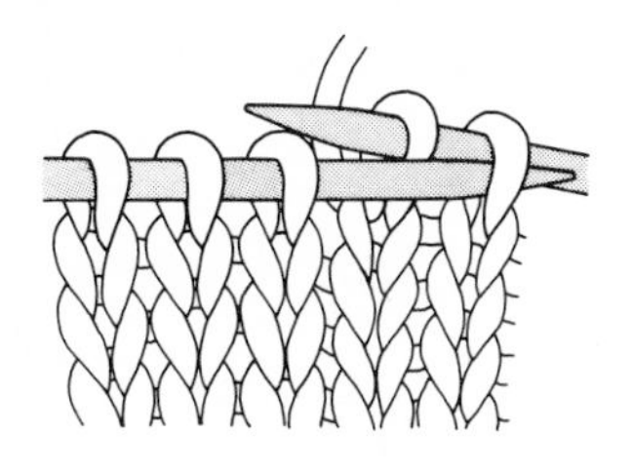

2. put the left needle into the first stitch

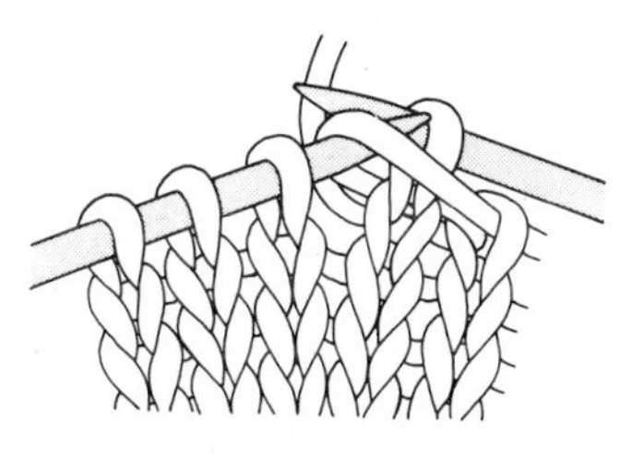

3. pull that stitch over the other stitch and

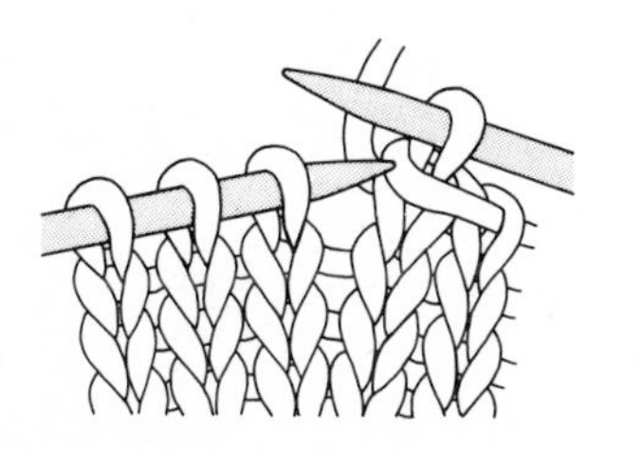

4. slip off the first stitch. Now you have cast off one stitch. Knit the next stitch, then continue from 2.

5. When you get to the last stitch, cut the yarn and pull the end through the last stitch.

TO DECREASE

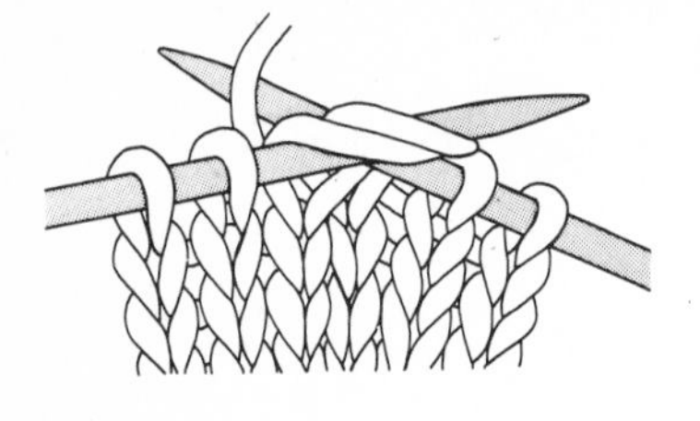

1. Put the right-hand needle through *two* stitches on the left-hand needle. Knit these two stitches together, in the usual way.

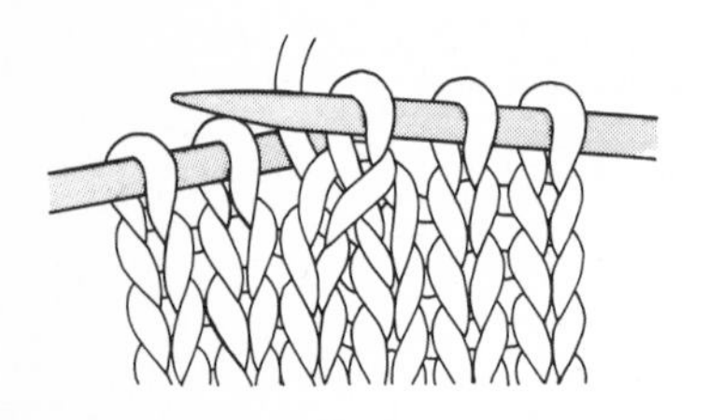

2. You have now decreased one stitch.

You can use this method to shape tops of skirts, trousers, socks, etc.

TO INCREASE

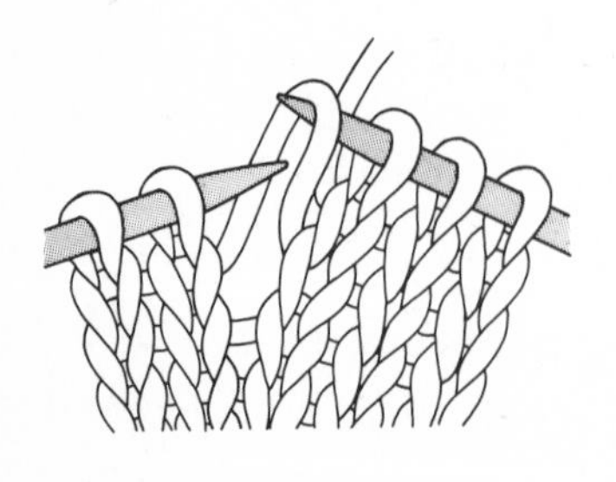

1. Put the right-hand needle through the loop that lies between the two stitches.

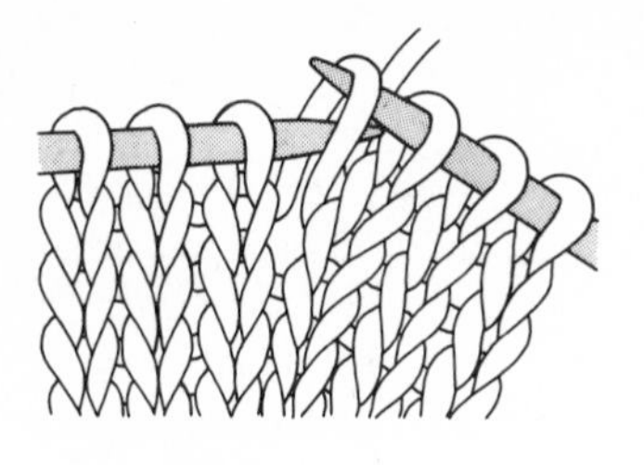

2. Put the left-hand needle through the loop.

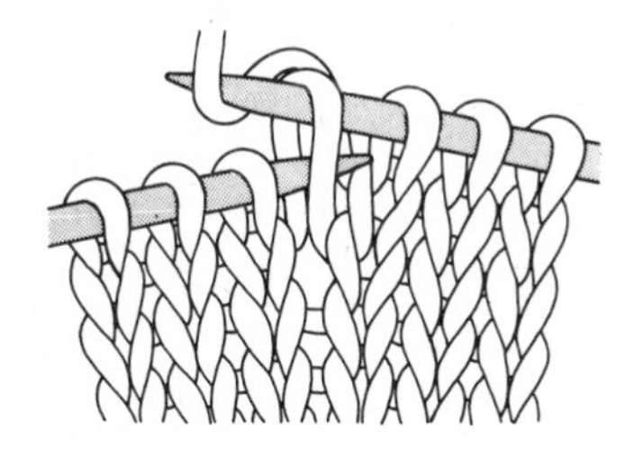

3. Put the yarn round the right-hand needle.

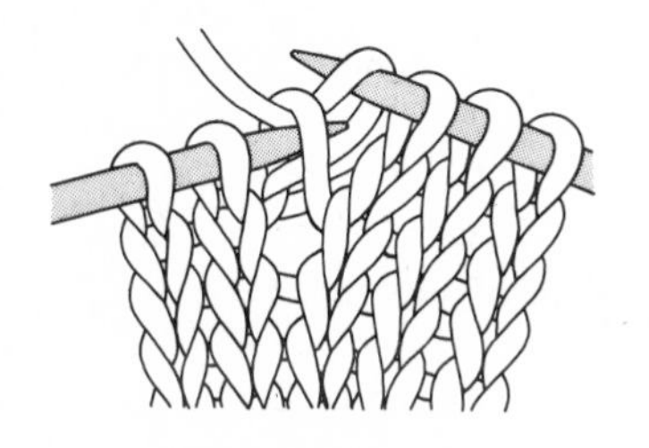

4. Pull a loop through like this.

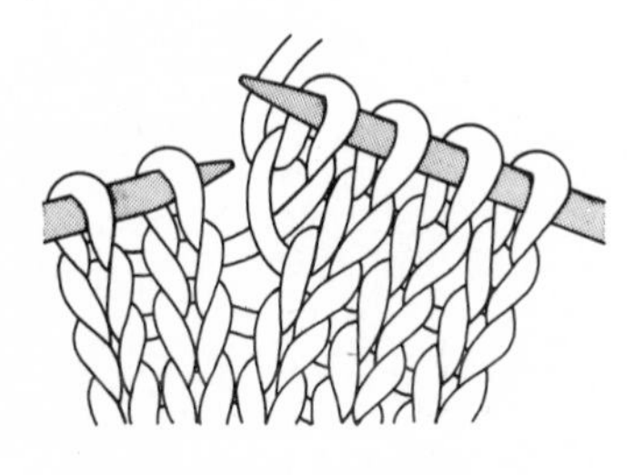

5. Let the picked-up loop drop from the needle. You have now increased one stitch.

Use this method to increase on all kinds of garments.

SEAMS

One of the advantages of circular knitting is that you need to sew very few seams when you've finished knitting; indeed some garments knitted by this method need no seaming – for example, gloves.

However, sewing the necessary seams carefully *is* important as bad seaming can badly spoil the look of a piece of knitting you've maybe spent weeks on.

There are three main methods of seaming: back stitch, flat seam and invisible seam. When sewing any of these use a large needle with a blunt point and the yarn used to knit the garment. If the yarn is very thick, you can split it to sew the seam.

BACK STITCH

This stitch forms a strong seam which is suitable for use where you want a non-stretch seam – it should be used for sewing together the shoulder seams on a heavy sweater for instance.

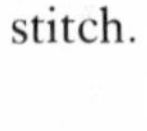

The seam should be about $\frac{1}{4}$ in. from the edge of the work. Put the two pieces of knitting together, right sides facing. Start the seam by sewing a double stitch through one edge. Beginning from the front, push the needle through the two thicknesses of knitting about $\frac{1}{8}$ in. to the right of where the yarn appears from the seam. The needle is now underneath; now push the needle about $\frac{1}{8}$ in. to the left of where the yarn appears from the seam so that the needle is now on the top. Pull the thread through.

Repeat until you have finished the seam. Fasten off with a double stitch.

Back-stitch seam

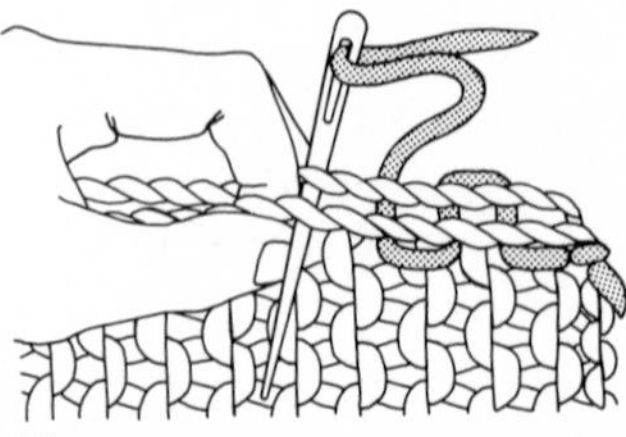

Flat seam

FLAT SEAM

As its name suggests, this seam is flat and does not produce a ridge. It is very useful for seaming ribbing or garter stitch knitting since it does not affect the elasticity of the stitch and doesn't cause an uncomfortable ridge where the knitting may be tight, for example at the neck or wrist.

Put the two edges together, right sides facing. Fasten the yarn to the underside with a double stitch. Then put the needle through the corresponding stitch on the upper edge. Pull the yarn through both stitches. Push the needle through the next stitch on the upper edge and through the corresponding stitch on the underside. Pull the thread through.

Repeat until the seam is completed. Fasten off with a double stitch.

You can of course use a back stitch and a flat seam in combination – for instance in a sleeve seam where you would sew the ribbing at the cuff with a flat seam and the stocking stitch with a back-stitch seam.

INVISIBLE SEAM

This is very useful for sewing garments where you want to avoid a thick seam, for example, sweaters knitted in a fine yarn, or tight-fitting socks.

Butt the two pieces, right sides uppermost. Fasten the thread to the lower edge of one of the pieces of knitting using a double stitch. Pick up one stitch from just opposite on the other edge. Pull the thread through tightly and push the needle through the next stitch on the opposite side.

Repeat until you have finished the seam, fastening off with a double stitch.

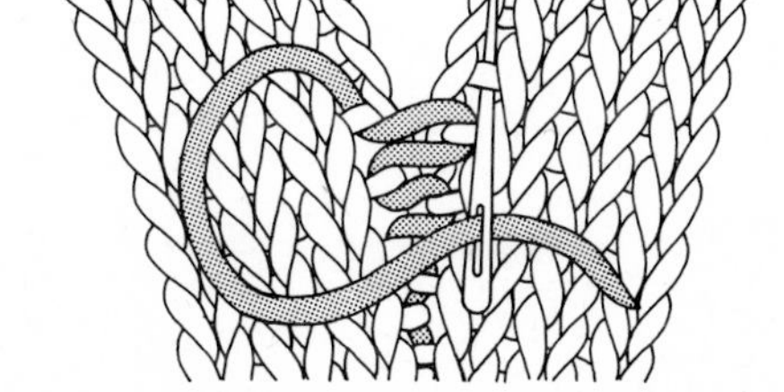

Invisible seam

CROCHET EDGING

Single or double crochet makes a strong, neat edging for knitting. For both you work into the stitches on the edge of the knitting, one by one, right to left.

TO JOIN YARN TO THE EDGE OF THE KNITTING

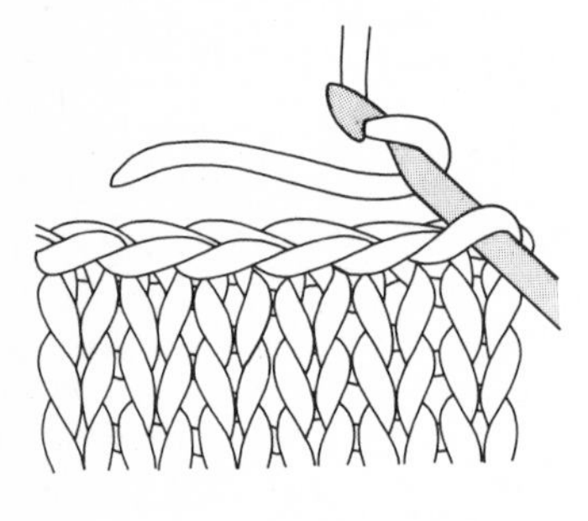

1. Insert hook through first knitted stitch, from front to back. Wind yarn around hook.

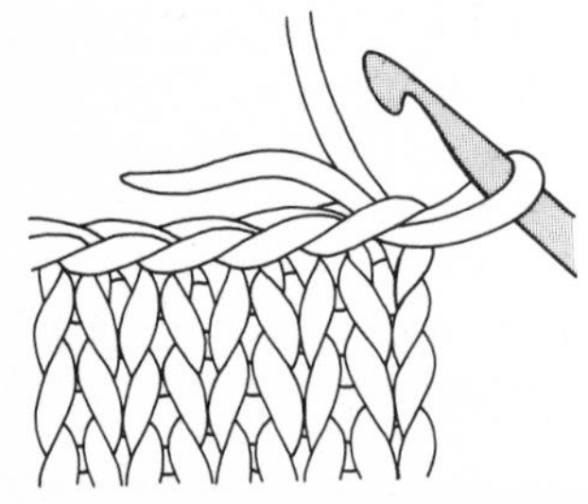

2. Pull loop through stitch.

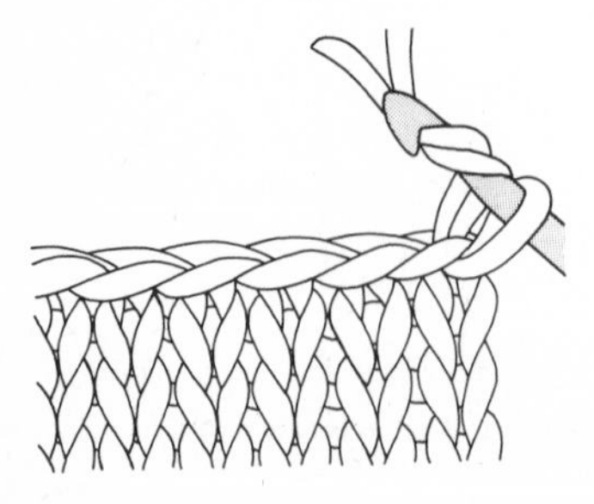

3. Wind yarn (doubled) around hook again, and pull this second loop through first.

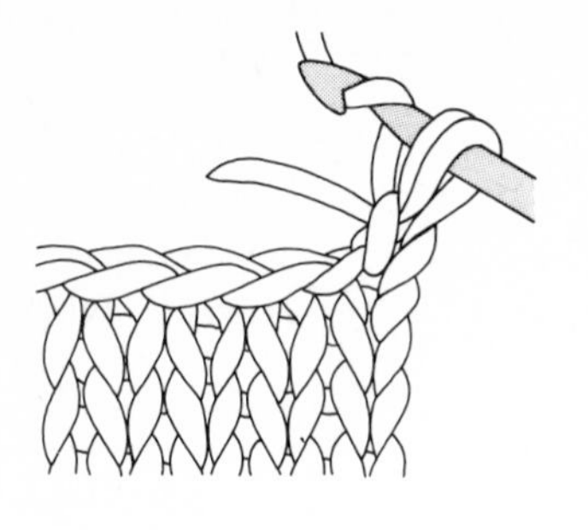

4. The yarn is now joined to the first stitch of the knitting.

SINGLE CROCHET

You have attached the wool on the first stitch as on page 104.

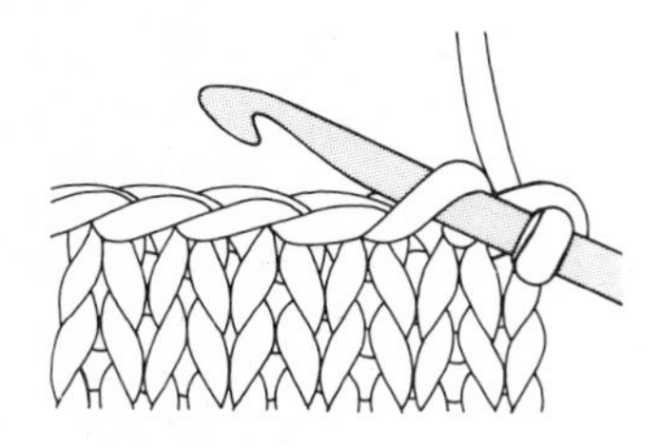

1. Insert hook from front to back into second knitted stitch,

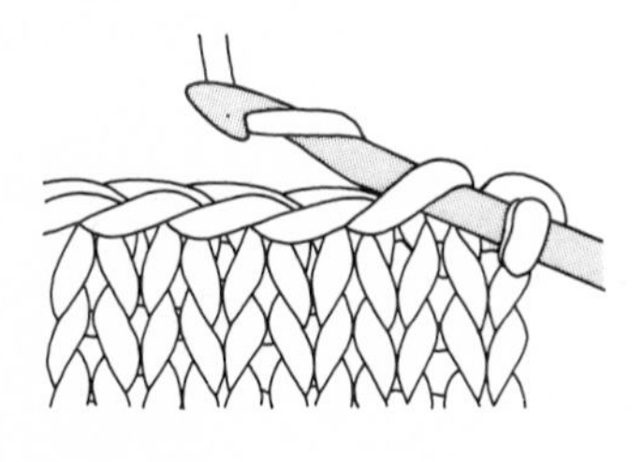

2. wind yarn around hook from right to left and

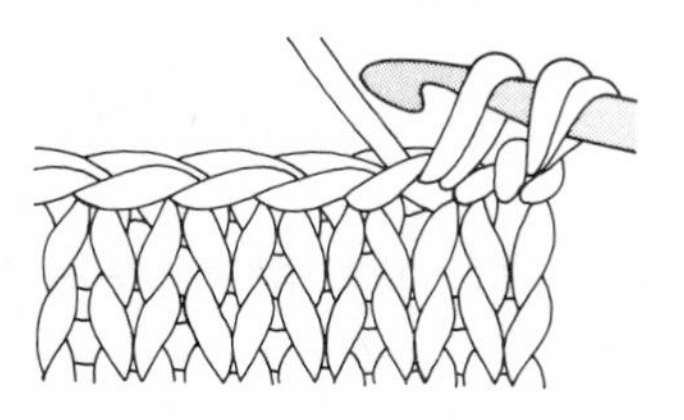

3. draw the loop through the knitted stitch. You now have two loops on the hook.

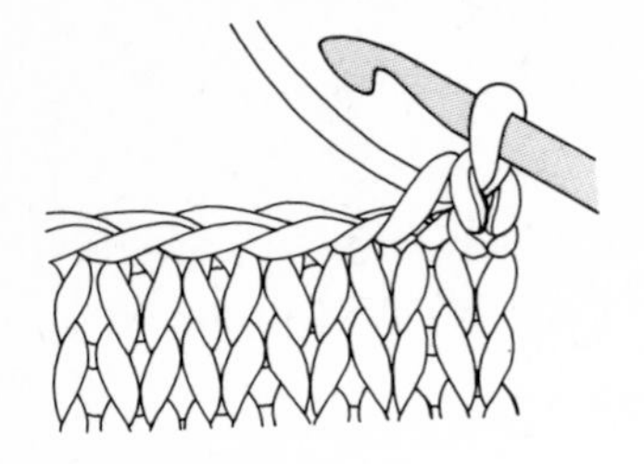

4. Wind the yarn round the hook and draw it through both loops. That's one complete single crochet. Continue along edge, making one single crochet in each knitted stitch.

Single crochet can also be used for buttonholes.

DOUBLE CROCHET

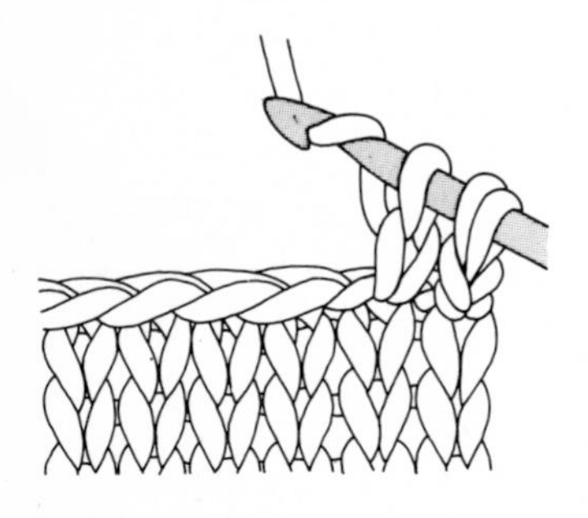

Join yarn to edge of knitting as on page 104, then follow instructions for single crochet up to 3. Then, instead of drawing yarn through both loops on hook, draw through one only, then wind yarn round hook again and pull through the two loops left on hook.

That's a complete double crochet. Continue along edge, making one double crochet in each knitted stitch.

CHAIN STITCH

This can be used for a drawstring.

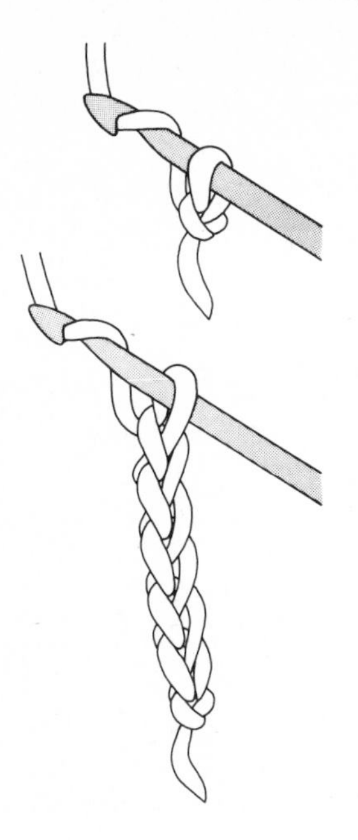

Make a loop on the hook, wind the yarn round the hook and draw this through the loop. Continue working chain to the required length.

Yarns

SHEEP BREEDING IN NORTH ZEALAND

Knitting by hand, as well as being an enjoyable way of passing the time, frees us from our dependence on shops with their emphasis on high-priced 'fashion'. As you knit more of your own clothes you may well want to become less dependent on retailers of knitting yarn and want to spin your own wool.

To find out about keeping sheep I interviewed a neighbour:

We began keeping sheep when we bought our first thousand acres of land. You can farm sheep while doing another job – I'm a lawyer – since the sheep almost take care of themselves. They have to have hay every day in winter and water when they lamb in early spring; the rest of the year they take care of their own water consumption while grazing. During the lambing season the sheep have to have a warm place with dry hay where they can shelter the lambs if it gets too cold and windy for them.

The sheep shearer comes once a year in June. When we began he got our wool as payment for his work. After a while we wanted to use our own wool – especially when we discovered that the shearer sold the wool to English spinners, who sell the wool back to Denmark in the form of high-priced knitting yarns.

'We send our wool to Laesø where it is either spun in one-, two-, three- or four-ply yarn or left unspun. We dye the white yarn ourselves with batik dyes which give soft shades. The unspun yarn can only be knitted by hand because it is so soft it breaks very easily. To make it workable we have to wind it together in two or three strands. Because we have lots of wool and so don't have time to knit all of it by hand, we have a knitting machine on which we knit sweaters in one evening, using the spun wool.

The whole family knits. Our elder daughter knits hats to her own designs and earns her pocket money by selling them to friends at school. Trine, who is nine, crochets lots of dolls' clothes. My husband has also started to knit – it was his New Year's resolution. On 1st January he said 'Teach me to knit'; on 2nd January he could knit and by February he had knitted two sweaters. He says it would be nice to have some knitting to do during the many tedious meetings he attends.

SPINNING

Unlike my friend, few people have enough land on which to keep sheep, but anyone can spin their own yarn.

There are various sources of wool for spinning. Art Needlework Industries will supply ready-combed undyed wool for spinning, or you could try asking where you see sheep grazing. You don't have to spin with wool – you could use your own hair, though it's a bit difficult to knit with as it slides so easily. (Don't cut your hair – collect the hairs from your brush and comb.) Dog hairs can be spun successfully – again, collect the hair the dog sheds naturally.

If you become interested in spinning, you may want to invest in a spinning wheel, but for your first attempts you can use the following method, which was used before the spinning wheel was invented.

1. The wool must first be carded (combed) to make it loose and even. You can thin it with your fingers if a friend holds one end of the clump of wool. The wool is now ready to be spun.
2. To make a simple spinning machine, take a round heavy object with a hole in the middle – for example, a piece of dried clay – a hook and a stick. Fix the hook into one end of the stick and slide the stick through the hole in the clay.
3. Twist the wool in your fingers. Knot the short thread you've made around the stick. Wrap the thread around the hook a couple of times.
4. Holding the stick between your legs, pull the wool out with your fingers to spin it. Hold the thread in your right hand and thin out more of the wool by pulling it out with your left hand. When you

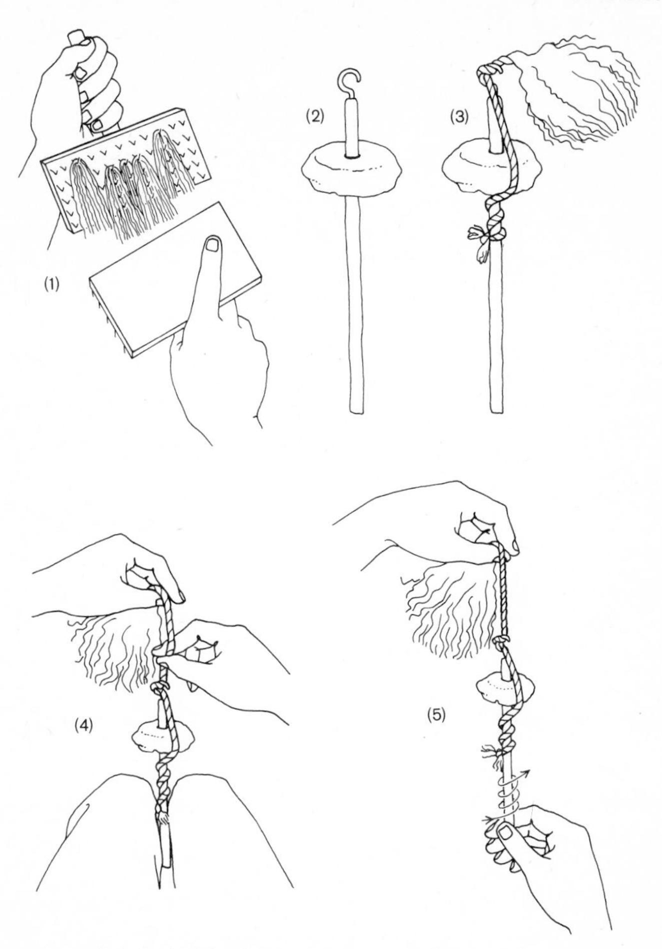

are sure the thread is thin enough let go with your right hand – be very careful here since if you let go before the wool is thin enough it will spin into a tight lumpy ball.

5. Hold the yarn thread with your left hand and the bottom of the stick with your right. Spin the spindle with your right hand. The wool is now yarn. When you've spun a long thread, unwind it from the hook and wrap it around the stick at the bottom of the spindle. Wind the thread round the hook and repeat the whole process.

RETAIL YARN SUPPLIERS

If you don't want to spin, you can of course buy yarn from retailers. Major spinners have retail outlets in chain stores, markets and specialist wool shops, but in case of difficulty I have listed the spinners' addresses below. Some have distributors in Australia, New Zealand, Canada and South Africa – these addresses are given on pages 113–14 – other spinners should be contacted at the UK address. I've also briefly described the kind of yarns the spinner produces, plus any specialities. Unless otherwise stated, all spinners will supply shade cards, but will only supply direct to the trade. If you would like to buy their yarns mail order, you can do so through the Needlewoman Shop, Regent Street, London W1.

Emu Wools Ltd, Leeds Road, Greengates, Bradford, Yorkshire. 4 ply, double knitting and chunky yarns in pure wool; same qualities plus baby yarns in acrylic and nylon; synthetic glitter yarns; mohair and synthetic mixtures.

Hayfield Textiles Ltd, Hayfield Mills, Glusburn, Keighley, Yorkshire. 4 ply, double knitting and chunky yarns in Bri-nylon, nylon, Courtelle, Terylene mixtures; same qualities in wool and synthetic mixtures; chunky wools in pure wool. Only supply shade cards to retailers.

George Lee and Sons Ltd and *Lister and Co Ltd*, both at PO Box 37, Providence Mills, Wakefield, Yorkshire. 4 ply, double knitting and chunky yarns in pure wool; same qualities in Courtelle, Bri-nylon, Tricel mixtures; mohair and synthetic mixtures.

Patons and Baldwins Ltd, PO Box 22, Darlington, County Durham. Baby wools, 4 ply, double knitting and chunky yarns in pure wool; baby wools, 4 ply and double knitting yarns in wool and synthetic mixtures; fancy yarns in angora, mohair and synthetic mixtures.

Robin Wools Ltd, Robin Mills, Idle, Bradford, Yorkshire. 4 ply, double knitting and chunky in pure wool; same qualities plus baby wool in nylon, Tricel, Courtelle and Bri-nylon; synthetic and wool mixtures; Courtelle crochet yarn; the Bernat Klein collection: pure wool bouclé, Shetland wool, fancy cotton (cotton and acrylic), mohair loop (mohair, wool and nylon).

Sirdar Ltd, PO Box 31, Alverthorpe, Wakefield, Yorkshire. 4 ply and double knitting in pure wool; nylc n yarn; Courtelle and wool mixtures.

3 Suisses Knityarns, Filature de L'Espierres, 13 Saffron Way, Leicester. 100 per cent Courtelle yarns; mixtures of synthetic and wool. Distribute Martin Mahoney's Blarney bainin, which is pure Irish wool. Will supply yarns by mail order if you don't live near one of their retail outlets.

H. G. Twilley Ltd, Roman Mill, Stamford, Lincolnshire. Several kinds of pure cotton yarn. Lurex and bouclé yarns.

OVERSEAS OUTLETS

Australia

Hayfield, Broseley Imports, 37 Chermside Street, Highgate Hill, Brisbane 4101.

Lee and Lister, M. J. Shaw and Co, 248 La Perouse Street, Red Hill, ACT 2603.

Patons, Coates Patons (Australia) Ltd, 321–55 Ferntree Gull Road, PO Box 110, Mount Waverly, Victoria 3149.

Sirdar, Sirdar Wools Pty Ltd, PO Box 472, Goulburn, New South Wales.

Twilley, Panda Yarns Ltd, Panda House, 48–56 Westin Street, Brunswick.

New Zealand

Lee and Lister, Fraser Napier and Co Ltd, 7th floor, World Trade Centre, Sturdee Street, Wellington.

Patons, Coates Patons Ltd, PO Box 6149, 48–52 Wyndham Street, Auckland 1.

Sirdar, Sirdar Division, Holeproof Mills Ltd, CPO Box 2216, Auckland.

Twilley, Mosgiel Ltd, Roslyn Mills Division, Kaikai Valley Road, Dunedin.

Canada

Lee and Lister, Dutex Co Ltd, 1520 Antonio Barbeau, Montreal, 355 PQ.

Sirdar, Diamond Yarn Corporation, 9697 St Lawrence Boulevard, Montreal, PQ.

Twilley, S.R. Kertzer and Co Ltd, 257 Adelaide Street West, Toronto.

South Africa

Lee and Lister, Lister and Co Pty Ltd, PO Box 1772, Cape Town.

Patons, Patons and Baldwins Pty Ltd, PO Box 33, Randfontein, Transvaal.

Sirdar, Sirdar Wools Pty Ltd, PO Box 4313, Johannesburg.

Twilley, The Monica Novelty Co Ltd, 139 President Street, Johannesburg 2000.

MAIL-ORDER YARN SUPPLIERS

The following companies will supply yarns mail order – most will dispatch orders to addresses throughout the world. They are obviously useful if you don't have a retailer near by, but they have an added advantage in that their yarns are cheaper than those in the shops. Catalogues and shade cards are supplied on request. Orders over a certain amount are sent post-free, and some companies will give discounts on bulk orders.

Art Needlework Industries Ltd, 7 St Michael's Mansions, Ship Street, Oxford. Coloured and undyed bainin wools from Ireland; Lopi wools from Iceland; handspun Harris tweed; Shetland wool; carded wool ready for spinning and dyeing.

Falcon Knitting Wools, R. S. Duncan and Co, Falcon Mills, Bartle Lane, Bradford, Yorkshire. Pure wool 4 ply and double knitting; synthetics in same qualities; alpaca (from llama) and wool mixes in natural undyed colours.

Holmfirth Wools, Briggate, Windhill, Shipley, Yorkshire. 4 ply, double knitting and chunky yarns in pure wool; wool/synthetics and 100 per cent synthetic yarns in same qualities.

Jamieson and Smith, 90 North Road, Lerwick, Shetland Isles. Sell only native wool from Shetland Isles in 2 ply and 3 ply. Wool is spun by Hunters of Brora on the mainland of Scotland.

Kiwi Wool Company, 32 Rebecca Street, Bradford, Yorkshire. 4 ply, double knitting and chunky in pure wool; synthetic yarns in same qualities; 100 per cent Shetland yarns; cotton crochet yarns.

Knitting Wools (Bradford) Ltd, 1 Cater Street, Bradford. 4 ply, double knitting and chunky yarns in pure wool; same qualities in synthetics and synthetic/wool mixtures; 100 per cent Shetland wool yarns.

Mailyarns, 38 High Street, Syston, Leicestershire. Will only supply within the UK. Nylon cord for knitting and crochet; 4 ply synthetic yarns; pure wool Aran yarns.

St John's Wools, PO Box 55, 39 Well Street, Bradford, Yorks. 4 ply, double knitting and chunky yarns in pure wool; same qualities in synthetics and synthetic/wool mixtures.

Scotnord Import Export Ltd. Distribute Lopi Iceland Fleece, made in Iceland by Alafoss from Iceland mountain sheep's wool. Can be obtained by mail order from Saga Mail Order, 29 King Street, Crieff, Perthshire.

Silverknit, Department B, Edwalton, Nottinghamshire. 2 ply, 3 ply and 4 ply yarns in both pure wool and synthetics.

Wool Fashion Bureau PO Box 16, Wakefield, Yorkshire. Double knitting and chunky yarns in pure wool; 4 ply, baby yarns and double knitting in synthetics.

Knitting Needle and Crochet Hook Sizes

KNITTING NEEDLE SIZES

English	Metric (mm)	USA
14	2·00	00
13	2·25	0
12	2·75	1
11	3·00	2
10	3·25	3
—	—	4
9	3·75	5
8	4·00	6
7	4·50	7
6	5·00	8
5	5·50	9
4	6·00	10
3	6·50	10½
2	7·00	11
1	7·50	13
0	8·00	—
00	9·00	—
000	10·00	—

CROCHET HOOK SIZES

	International (mm)	Old size
	7·00	2
	6·00	4
	5·50	5
	5·00	6
	4·50	7
	4·00	8
	3·50	9
	3·00	10 11
	2·50	12
	2·00	14

MEASUREMENTS: METRIC AND IMPERIAL EQUIVALENTS

Metric	Imperial
1 cm	just under ½ in.
5 cm	2 ins.
10 cm	4 ins.
20 cm	8 ins.
50 cm	20 ins.
100 cm	39 ins.

Imperial	Metric
½ in.	1·3 cm
1 in.	2·5 cm
5 ins.	12·5 cm
10 ins.	25·0 cm
36 ins.	91·0 cm
49 ins.	102·0 cm

John Bull

FAIRISLE PATTERNS

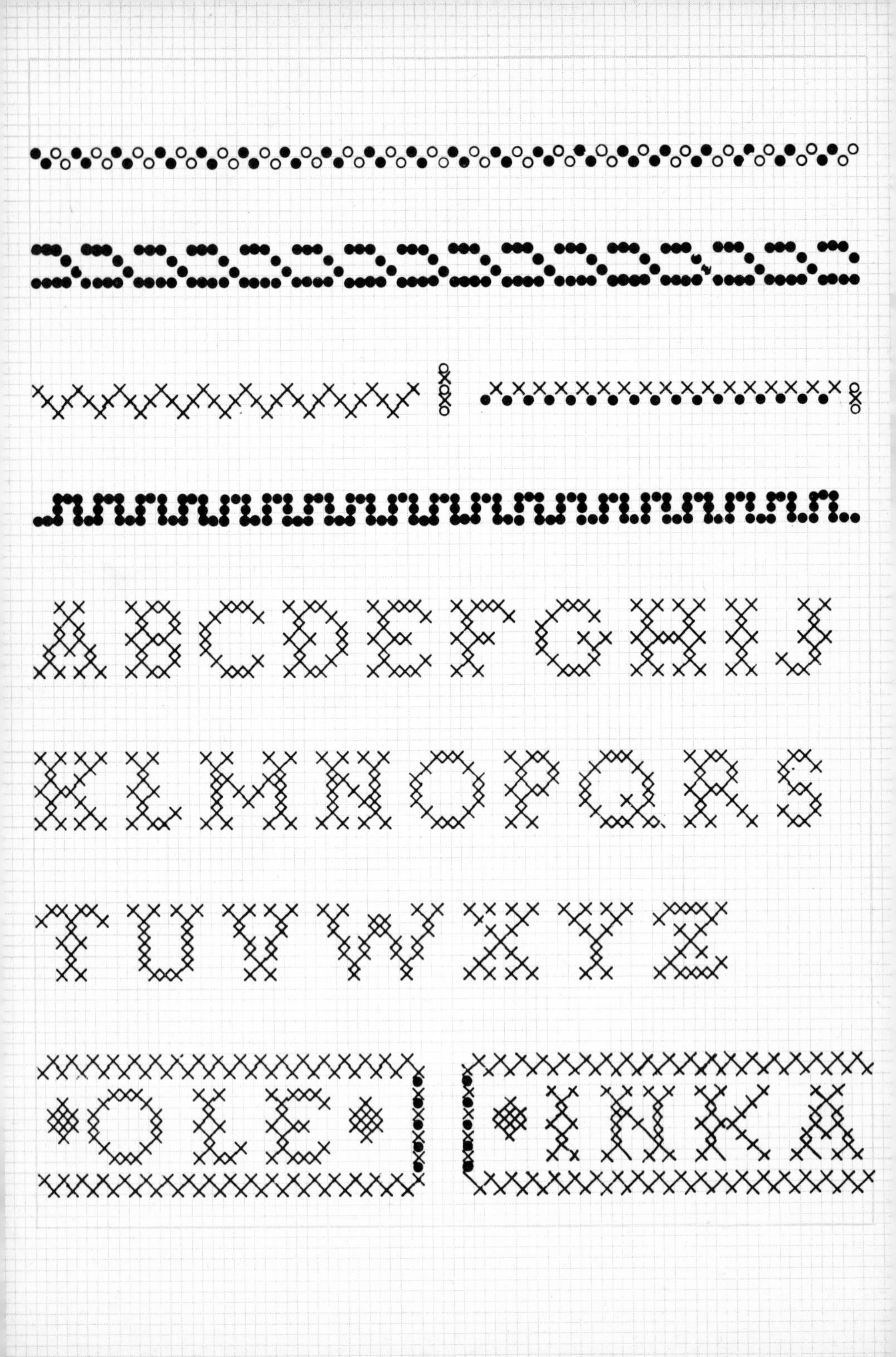
A B C D E F G H I J
K L M N O P Q R S
T U V W X Y Z
OLE
INKA

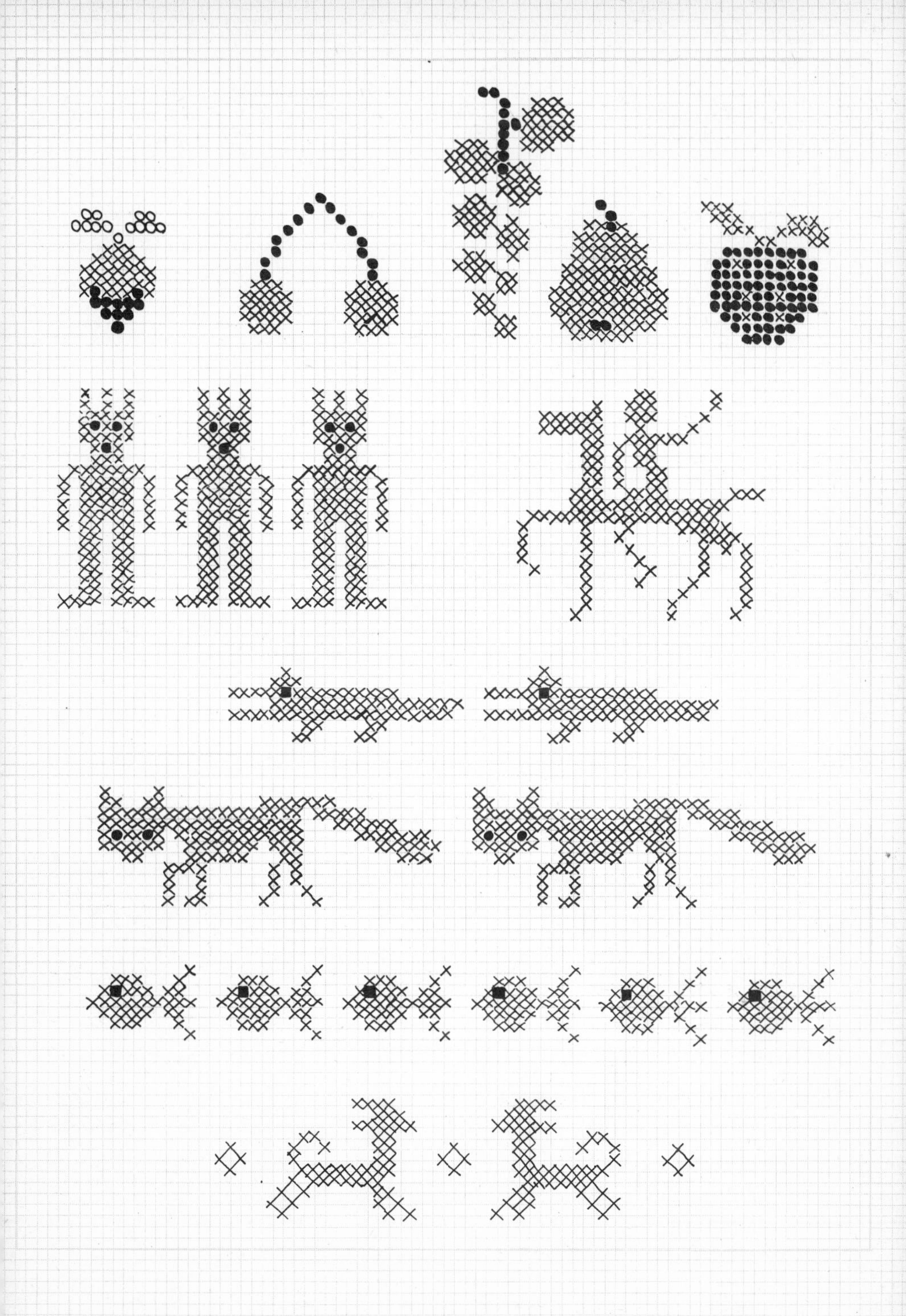

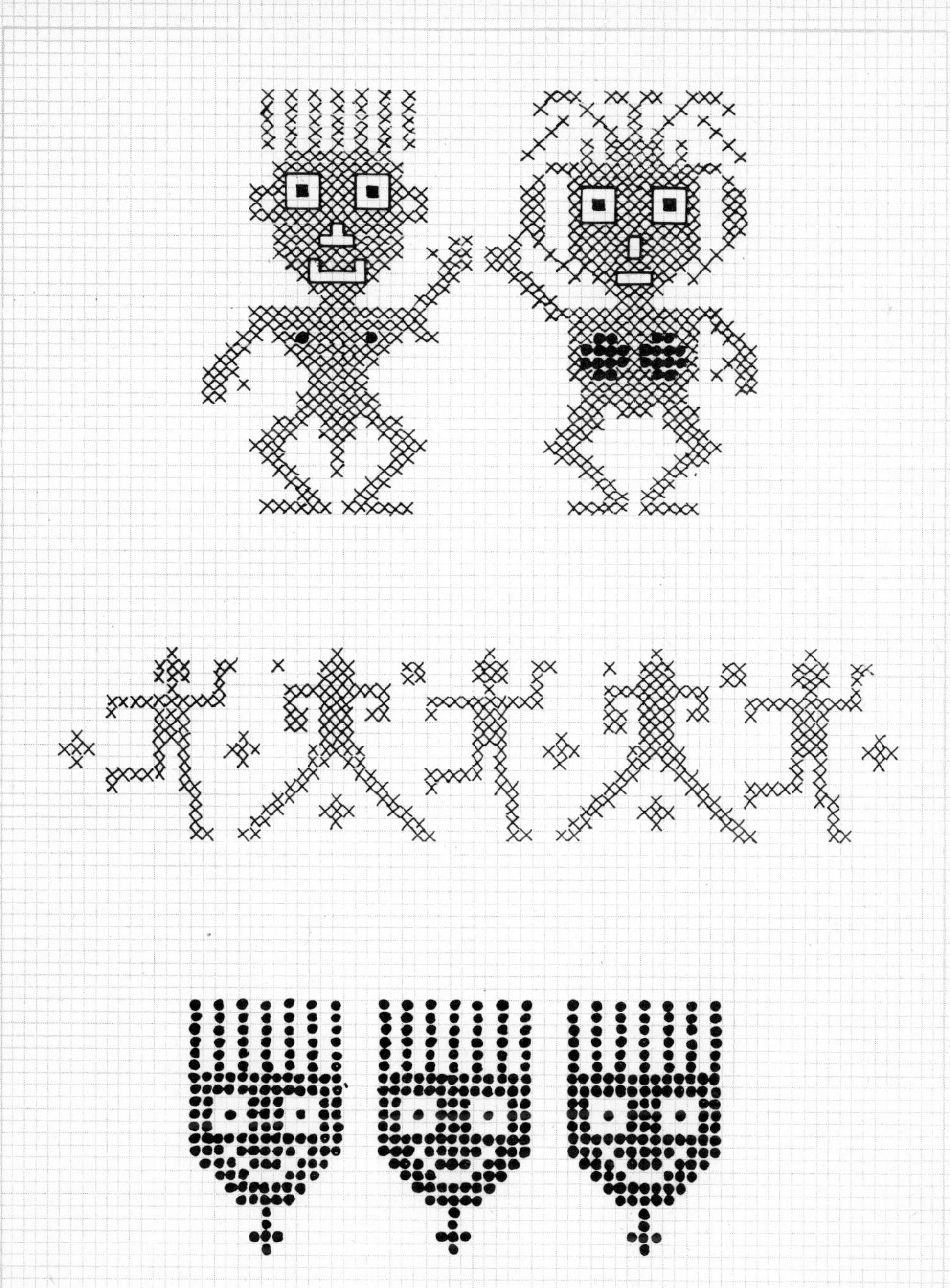